Class Lives

CLASS LIVES

Stories from across
Our Economic Divide

Edited by

Chuck Collins, Jennifer Ladd,
Maynard Seider, and Felice Yeskel

A CLASS ACTION BOOK

ILR Press
an imprint of

CORNELL UNIVERSITY PRESS
ITHACA AND LONDON

First published 2014 by Cornell University Press
First printing, Cornell Paperbacks, 2014
Printed in the United States of America

Library of Congress Cataloging-in-Publication Data

    Class lives : stories from across our economic divide / edited by Chuck Collins, Jennifer Ladd, Maynard Seider, and Felice Yeskel.
      pages cm
    "A Class Action book."
    Includes bibliographical references and index.
    ISBN 978-0-8014-5328-1 (cloth : alk. paper) —
    ISBN 978-0-8014-7965-6 (pbk. : alk. paper)
    1. Class consciousness—United States. 2. Social classes—United States. 3. Intergroup relations—United States. I. Collins, Chuck, 1959– editor of compilation. II. Ladd, Jennifer, 1952– editor of compilation. III. Seider, Maynard, 1943– editor of compilation. IV. Yeskel, Felice, editor of compilation. V. Class Action (Organization), sponsoring body.
    HN90.S6C5646   2014
    305.50973—dc23   2014014501

Cloth printing   10 9 8 7 6 5 4 3 2 1
Paperback printing   10 9 8 7 6 5 4 3 2 1

Contents

PART III. MIDDLE CLASS

PART IV. OWNING CLASS

PART V. MIXED CLASS

Class Lives

Introduction

Caviar, College, Coupons, and Cheese

BY FELICE YESKEL

C lass is the last great taboo in the United States. It is, according to Noam Chomsky, "the unmentionable five-letter word."

Even in this period of growing economic inequality, we hardly ever talk about class. We hear daily, in the mainstream media, about unemployment, bailouts, proposed tax cuts or tax hikes, Congress regulating one industry and deregulating another, budget cuts, recession, recovery, roller-coaster markets, CEO bonuses, and more. Given all the attention to economics, it is interesting that talk about social class has been so skimpy.

Sometimes I think of class as our collective, national family secret. And, as any therapist will tell you, family secrets are problematic. With rare exceptions, we just don't talk about class in the United States. Most of us believe that the United States is a classless society, one that is basically middle class (except for a few unfortunate poor people and some lucky rich ones). Sometimes talk about class is really about race. We have no shared language about class. We have been taught from childhood myths and misconceptions around class mobility and the American dream.

Many of us are confused about class and don't tend to think about it as consciously as we might our race, ethnicity, gender, religion, age, or sexual orientation. Nonetheless, our class identity has a huge impact on every aspect of our lives: from parenting style to how we speak, from what we dare to dream to the likelihood we will spend time in prison, from how we spend our days to how many days we have.

We are living in a period of extraordinary economic insecurity and inequality. It is an inequality that crushes the poor, drains the working class, eliminates the middle class, simultaneously aggrandizes and dehumanizes the rich, and disembowels democracy.

My Story of Class Awakening

Since many of us grew up in neighborhoods with an amazing amount of class segregation, we often didn't notice class differences. I have met plenty of folks who grew up quite poor or quite wealthy who never noticed, since everyone around them was the same. They felt "normal." It's often when we cross class boundaries that we notice the differences.

My own class awakening came fairly early in life. When I was five years old, I was sent from my neighborhood in New York City to Hunter College Elementary School on Sixty-Eighth Street and Park Avenue, a school for "intellectually gifted" kids. I not only crossed the miles on the way to school, but the cultures too. The fact that almost all the kids at Hunter were white like me obscured deep differences among us. I learned to act differently, talk differently, and basically to pass as middle class. I never invited anyone home from school because I was ashamed of where I lived. I did, however, visit Park Avenue penthouses where I worried that my very presence might make something dirty.

For work my dad bought used burlap and cotton sacks, the ones that held one hundred pounds of flour, from bagel and bialy bakeries. He came home from work each day caked in flour and sweat. When I asked him what I should tell people when they asked what he did, he said, "bagman." But even as a young kid, I knew I didn't want to say that. He said I could also say "peddler," since he bought the sacks from the bakeries and then sold them to be recycled. I wasn't sure "peddler" was much better.

My mom sold advertising over the phone, which she called "telephone sales." Neither of my parents had gone to college, nor had most of their friends. My school friends all had dads who were professionals, and their moms (if they worked outside the home) were professionals too. No one ever discussed this difference; it dared not speak its name. But I did acutely feel the difference, and its name was class.

After elementary school, I won a scholarship to a New York City private school (now called an independent school). I already had my school uniform and was ready to start seventh grade when I told my parents I didn't want to go to the fancy school, I wanted to be a regular kid and go to my local public school. My social needs prevailed, so I attended public schools through high school on Manhattan's Lower East Side. While I gave up some benefits academically, I think I made the right emotional choice, because I finally had friends with whom I felt comfortable.

After being the first in my family to go to college, I decided to earn a doctorate in social justice education. I had been involved in teaching about issues of social identity and the social forces that impact the unjust and inequitable distribution of resources, opportunity, and recognition. I use the term "social justice education" rather than diversity or multiculturalism, because social justice education explicitly addresses the issue of differential access to social power in addition to difference.

When I started my graduate program in social justice education there were others who were teaching and developing curricular materials on racism and sexism; work on anti-Semitism, heterosexism, and ableism followed next. But almost no one included the issue of classism. Social class identity was not discussed, nor was oppression based on social class or perceived social class. The issue of classism was not on the agenda for the academy or for most activists, although there were some great writings, mostly from the feminist community.

My experience of having a foot in two different class realities, or being bicultural with respect to class, led to my ongoing engagement with these issues and my decision in the mid-1980s to write my doctoral dissertation on teaching about issues of class and classism.

I explored various academics' perspectives on class. Some talked about class in terms of occupational status, blue/pink collar or white collar, work with the hands or work with the head. I could look up a job title and find out how much prestige or status is associated with that occupation. Some, on the other hand, talked about class in purely economic terms. This framework meant that income or wealth identifies people's class strata: for instance, does their income or wealth place them in the bottom quintile or the middle quintile?

Economists and sociologists with a classical Marxist perspective talked more about power, ownership, and control—who owns the means of production and who sells their labor. According to this view, the vast majority of us are working class selling our labor power—even highly paid physicians, losing control over the conditions under which they labor, with managed care creating a new type of professional assembly line. Theoretically this made sense to me, but I wondered if to the average person a well-paid doctor had a lot in common class-wise with someone flipping burgers.

I found others who looked at class as attitudes, behavior, lifestyle, values, consumption, or culture. Average people often read class into whether someone drinks beer vs. white wine, lattes at independent coffee shops vs. coffee at Dunkin' Donuts.

I imagined two white men in their early thirties. The first, wearing a jacket and tie, works in an office and spends his day at a desk in front of a computer and talking on the telephone, goes home, pours himself a glass of white wine, and listens to NPR. He earns $30,000 a year. The second man pulls on a pair of coveralls, picks up his tools, and spends his day making house calls as a plumber; when he goes home he opens a can of beer and watches TV. He earns $59,000 a year. Although worker number two brings home almost twice the income of the first worker, most folks would think that worker one is middle class and worker two is working class. It would seem that money alone doesn't tell the whole story about class.

In short, there was no agreed-upon definition of class. The complexity and multifaceted nature of class and classism became overwhelmingly clear to me. No wonder class was hard to talk about; we weren't even sure what we were talking about.

Luckily I realized before too long that although dealing with class was my life's work, it might not be right for my dissertation. I switched topics. However, I have spent the two decades since then exploring, educating, and organizing around classism and economic inequality.

Responding to Economic Inequality: Working to Change Policy

In 1994, with the economic divide continuing to widen, Chuck Collins and I founded a national nonprofit, United for a Fair Economy (UFE), which raises awareness about how concentrated wealth and power undermine our economy, corrupt democracy, deepen the racial divide, and tear communities apart.

During my years with UFE, I led hundreds of workshops about growing economic inequality. One of the most popular activities demonstrated wealth distribution in the United States by lining up ten chairs, with each chair representing one-tenth of the total privately owned wealth. We then asked for ten volunteers, with each person representing one-tenth of the total population.

As of 2010, the latest year for which figures are available from the Federal Reserve Board, the richest 10 percent of U.S. households owned 76.7 percent of the nation's private wealth, and the other 90 percent owned a combined total of 23.3 percent.[1] This vast inequality of wealth ownership became powerfully clear when one person stretched across seven chairs and the other nine people crowded onto three chairs. When I asked the person representing the wealthiest 10 percent if he had any advice for the other nine, suggestions in line with our nation's cherished myths would come forward: "work hard," "get a good education," "believe in yourself"—and occasionally a joking "choose the right family."

When I turned to the nine others crowded onto three chairs and asked their thoughts about their situation, their stereotypical responses tended to fall into one of three categories. First, self-blame, in a litany of "if onlies": "If only I'd stayed in school"; "If only I hadn't gotten pregnant"; "If only I'd majored in computer science and not English lit"; "If only I hadn't gotten divorced."

Next came blaming others, sometimes with some pushing and shoving—or, as I came to think of it, "scapegoat du jour": "It's those new immigrants taking our jobs"; "I worked hard for my chair, get your own chair"; "Welfare moms have all those kids—I don't want to pay higher taxes to support their laziness."

The last category was fantasy, or, as I came to think of it, buying lottery tickets: folks on the bottom identifying with the one person with seven chairs and believing that somehow, someday, they would be there.

---

1. Economic Policy Institute, *State of Working America*, 12th ed. (Cornell University Press, 2012), 379.

All these responses to the extreme wealth inequality in our society are some form of classism. The self-blame is internalized class inferiority, and the other-blame reflects a classist sense of superiority. Without systemic explanations for extreme inequality, people individualize, blaming or lauding individuals. While individual effort, intelligence, and risk-taking do play a role, as does luck, they tell only a small portion of the story.

Information about changes in tax policies, spending policies, wage policies, global competition, and the attacks on unions leading to decreased unionization, to name a few, fly beneath most folks' radar screens. Instead we maintain a set of beliefs and myths—an ideology—that explains and justifies a system that has created a widening gap between the haves and the rest of us.

The numbers make clear this country's level of extreme economic inequality. In 2010, the wealthiest 1 percent owned more wealth (35.4 percent) than the bottom 90 percent combined, and the total inflation-adjusted net worth of the Forbes 400 rose from $502 billion in 1995 to over $2 trillion in 2013.[2]

This extreme inequality is problematic in myriad ways. It is bad for our democracy, bad for our culture, and bad for our economy. As Supreme Court Justice Louis Brandeis observed, "We can have democracy in this country or great wealth concentrated in the hands of a few, but we can't have both." Extreme wealth generates extreme power—the power to shape political priorities and cultural norms.

Getting into the Felt Experience of Class and Classism

Although many policy changes would benefit the vast majority of the population, many people routinely vote against their economic self-interest. I remember telling the driver of a taxicab that I was flying to a conference to discuss economic inequality. While we talked, I explained changes in the tax code that benefited asset owners at the expense of wage earners. His response was that he didn't have a lot of

2. Wealth data: ibid., 379. Forbes 400: "Inside the *Forbes* 400," *Forbes*, September 16, 2013, http://www.forbes.com/sites/luisakroll/2013/09/16/inside-the-2013-forbes-400-facts-and-figures-on-americas-richest/.

money, but if he did, he wouldn't want anyone to tax it away. Although the chances this cabbie would end up in the top 1 percent are practically nil—as remote as winning the lottery—he identified not with his current reality, but up the class spectrum with his aspirations. Talking with him made clear to me again that just talking about changing economic policy was not enough. We had to change consciousness and ideology as well as policy.

Class is relative, and class is relational. Whom we compare ourselves to determines a lot about our subjective, or felt, experience of class. Many of us socialize with people who are relatively similar to us class-wise. Breaking down these barriers and getting to know others from very different places on the class spectrum are important to challenging assumptions, breaking stereotypes, and challenging class myths.

In 1995 Jenny Ladd, who comes from an owning-class background, and I decided to start a cross-class dialogue group. There were eight of us: four came from poor and working-class backgrounds, and four came from owning-class backgrounds, each with a million dollars of assets or more. The scope of monetary resources in the group ranged from $60,000 in medical debt to $14 million in assets.

For over six and a half years, we met for five hours monthly in each other's homes. We saw ourselves as a learning laboratory for understanding the dynamics of class. We shared a lot about our experiences, our hopes, fears, dreams, choices, lack of choices, guilt, anger, shame, and cluelessness. We told each other the amount of money we had, earned, gave away, saved, and spent. We examined the judgments we had of others, and the fears about others' judgments of us. After six and a half years, all of us felt transformed by our collective experience. Some of us took risks we had never thought possible: leaving safe jobs, moving across the country, giving away over half our wealth, refusing future inheritance, and saving for retirement.

Jenny and I wondered if we could bring some of what our cross-class experience had given to us into the world, even though most people wouldn't be likely to spend six and a half years in dialogue and reflection. We started a nonprofit organization in 2005 called Class Action, with the mission of inspiring action to end classism. We wanted to bring class issues into the realm of public conversation—assuming that, as consciousness is raised and language found to describe class experiences, people across the class spectrum would be more likely to want to change a system that is at odds with basic democratic values of equity, justice, and liberty for all.

One of our basic strategies was to educate people about issues of class and classism. We did this in a variety of ways. We developed workshops that we facilitated in educational, civic, religious, social service, and social change organizations.

In one of the activities we developed for our workshops, we asked participants to get into a single line based on their class of origin—from those who grew up in the "lowest class," to those who grew up in the "highest class."

Often folks would stare at us: asking how they were going to do that, or what was the definition of "class." We suggested they think about what they needed to know to decide where to put themselves on the line in relation to each other. After a few minutes of awkward silence, workshop participants would start to engage in lively conversation. After fifteen or twenty minutes we would ask participants to take their place on the line.

Once we had a single line, we would ask people to share their feelings about doing the activity and about where they were in the line. Often those at both ends of the line had the most intense feelings, such as pride, shame, anger, guilt, surprise, isolation, and anxiety. We would then ask everyone what were the factors or indicators that caused them to place themselves where they had. We collectively developed a list of class indicators.

Class indicators typically included the more "objective" measures such as parents' highest level of formal education, income, wealth, debt, occupation, home-ownership, and neighborhood. The much longer list of subjective indicators included language (accent, grammar, diction, volume, vocabulary), clothing (new or secondhand, cotton or polyester), posture or carriage, food, recreational activities, expectations, and values. People read class into just about everything

The class indicators also seemed to change depending on where on the class line we focused. For those at the bottom of the spectrum the indicators were about basic survival: was there enough food, or was there a roof over their head at night? As we moved up the class spectrum, indicators included stability of employment and housing, and what occupation or education parents had. Toward the middle, indicators turned to educational expectations, home-ownership, and vacations. Moving still higher, indicators included travel, multiple home ownership, private schools, and trust funds. At the very top, the most important indicators were who one's people were and one's family and social connections, including relation to royalty.

After doing this activity with hundreds of groups, we found that two of the most memorable indicators at different ends of the spectrum were "Did you use 'summer' as a verb?" at the top, and "Did you eat the cheese?" at the bottom. The cheese referred to is processed cheese that the U.S. government provided to welfare and food stamp recipients during the 1980s and early 1990s. If you ate the cheese, you know who you are. I selected this as one of the indicators in the title of this introduction.

After this activity, we asked participants to create small groups, class-of-origin caucuses, with others who occupied a similar place on the spectrum. Each caucus answered the same set of questions, including, What was good about your experience? What was hard about your experience? What questions do you have for another class group? What questions would you not want to be asked? What is a good name for your group? Groups gave themselves names like "True Grit," "Scrappy Survivors," "Bingo, Ball Games, and Beer," "Coupon Cutters and Casseroles," "Good Grades, College, and Practical Jobs," "Vanilla Wafers and Milk after School," "Volvos and Golden Retrievers," "Private Schools, European Vacations, and Trust Funds," "Nobility and Noblesse Obligers."

After each small group shared its responses with the whole group, we engaged in cross-class dialogue, with groups asking and answering questions. Workshop participants consistently reported that meeting and hearing the firsthand experiences of folks from very different life situations was transformative, and it motivated them to want to do something about classism.

When we do talk about class, we tend to talk only about the strengths of wealth and the limitations of poverty. But in reality it is much more complex. All of us derive strengths as well as limitations from our class position and experience. For example, working-class people learn resourcefulness and the ability to adapt to quickly changing circumstances. Some people raised in the owning class are paralyzed by an unexpected change or broken system. Because of intense class segregation in this country, few of us have the opportunity to learn about each other's strengths and to grow past our limitations. Cross-class connection is essential to regaining our full humanity.

Why an Anthology?

For many participants, the most powerful part of the workshop is hearing stories from others of similar and different classes. The similarities are validating: they allow people to see that what they thought was unique to their family may in fact be a larger phenomenon. The differences are illuminating, allowing small windows into different worlds.

Over the years, Class Action has reached tens of thousands of people through our website, school curricula, blogs, videos, pamphlets, articles, and workshops. But no matter how many people actually come to our workshops, meet folks from very different class positions, and reflect on how class impacts their lives and what they can do to work against classism, I know there are many thousands more who are hungering for ways to make sense of their class experiences. I hope this book will reach many of them.

Organization of the Book

With our title, *Class Lives,* we see "lives" as a verb as well as a noun. As a verb, it speaks to the power of class, impinging on all of us, whether we are aware of it or not. As a noun, it speaks to the goal of this anthology, to bring out the lives of forty individuals, from across the class spectrum, each unique, yet each very aware of the power of class.

I refer to the class indicators—caviar, college, coupons, and cheese—in this introduction to give a sense of four of the major class groups: caviar for the owning class, college for the middle class, coupons for the working class, and cheese for the poor. The stories included span the class spectrum, providing insight into issues of social class and how all of us are affected.

At the end you'll find a resource section, with information including books and websites to help you to further explore the relationship of class and society. Also included is the contributors' biographical information: some are previously published writers, many are members of academia, and many are activists. All share the sense of mission and purpose from which this anthology project was born.

There are limitations to this collection of stories. We have many stories from those who grew up poor, but few from folks who grew up poor and still live in poverty. Much, though not all, of our outreach was done through the Internet, and the digital divide certainly accounts for who heard our call and who didn't.

Poverty also suppresses voice. Oppression means we don't get to hear certain realities. People from backgrounds of poverty who have articulated their experience often have some access to privilege, either a parent from a higher class who supported them, more formal education, or more cross-class relationships. Often when someone is dealing with the day-to-day realities of survival, there is little time and energy to write, and little belief in an audience who wants to read about what poverty is really like.

We also lack stories from the super-wealthy or the ruling class. No one from the corporate or political elite felt comfortable sharing his story, or her story. Some considered publishing under a pseudonym, but even that anonymity proved too scary.

While we have several stories from Latinos and people of African descent, which span some of the class spectrum from poor to upper middle class, finding owning-class people of color willing to share their stories was difficult. We talked with several owning-class people of color, but coming out as a minority within a minority creates a super visibility that was too uncomfortable for them, so they decided not to contribute. We also were unable to recruit any stories from people of Asian or Native American background.

While there have been other collections of class stories, we don't think any have been as diverse as this one. We hope reading these stories will encourage you to share your story and to take action to make this a less classist society.

When Class Action envisions a world without classism, it is a world that

- meets everyone's basic needs;
- treats people from every background, class status, and rank with dignity and respect;

- supports the development of all people to their full potential;
- reduces the vast differences in income, wealth, and access to resources; and
- ensures that all people have a voice in the decisions that affect them.

Wouldn't you like to live in that world?

PART I

Poor and Low Income

TO BE POOR IN THE UNITED STATES OR CANADA is not just to be faced with material need on a daily basis, to be "born into the culture of hunger," to be homeless, or to live without indoor plumbing or electricity. With it comes negative judgment from others and feelings of shame. As one contributor put it: "I understood everything—that I was less, and they were more." Those feelings lead to attempts to hide one's stigmatized condition, while living in fear that one will be found out.

The number of people who are officially poor in the United States, by conservative federal standards, continues to rise and now stands at over 16 percent of the population. For children, the figure is even higher, at over 21 percent.[1]

Most of the contributors in this section were born poor, but one, Wendy Williams, became poor through divorce and a stepparent's unemployment. While all have moved out of poverty, the memories and feelings of their early years remain with them. For one, "Time and love and success have

---

1. U.S. Census, "Income, Poverty, and Health Insurance in the United States in 2012," http://www.census.gov/hhes/www/poverty/data/incpovhlth/2012/index.html.

come my way, but I still feel marked and conspicuous." For another, "I think about class all of the time."

The stories have much in common for these seven women, whether they came of age in the 1950s or the 1980s. Often the clothes and shoes they wore became the subject of ridicule from young classmates (and even, in one case, from a teacher) and marked them as being "less than." Or it could be the different-colored lunch ticket they used at school, or the lack of home address on the form, as there was no category labeled "homeless."

For those born without white-skin privilege, issues of racism added to the class stigma they faced. The complications increased for one Mexican American woman, Geneva Reynaga-Abiko, who, while growing up poor in California, was accused of being "rich" by her extended family back in Mexico. Later, when she became a highly educated and successful professional, her own family accused her of "being white" for leaving the neighborhood to live in a more upscale setting. As Geneva observes, "I often feel guilty for not returning to Fontana, where much of my family still lives," yet she is "confident that . . . they are unconsciously happy that I have been able to leave the crime-ridden city where we were all born. . . . I am sure they are proud of me."

Such ambivalent feelings mark the upward mobility of many of these women. As with Geneva, it may come with visits to family members who have not done as well as their daughters. Even at the height of a career as a widely recognized organizer, leader, and author, Linda Stout admits that "even now, sometimes one person's classist attitude can throw me back to that place of believing I'm not good enough, not smart enough, or strong enough."

We are reminded that these seven women are not a random or representative sample of women born into poverty, as we learn about their journeys to higher education, well-regarded careers, and, for most of them, adult material security. They gain their own strength in various ways: from loving parents, from supportive extended families, from peers who understood their pain, and from kindly teachers and cafeteria workers. They have learned resilience and resourcefulness. As Fisher Lavell writes about her rural Canadian family, "Survivorship is a gift of my poverty-class upbringing. Resiliency, the ability to take the blows and come up swinging. Empathy, generosity, an open heart; things you acquire from being rejected, doing without, and carrying a burden alone." For Linda Stout, a journey to Nicaragua helped her shift her understanding of poverty and to strengthen herself. There she "met people who acknowledged poverty, but who were proud of who they were. They were revolutionaries who knew that the poverty they suffered was a problem of the system—not their personal fault. I came back from that trip with a determination to 'come out of the closet' as a poor person."

And so we can read the many stories of those who have come out of the closet, who now live their authentic lives and engage in the struggle to fight classism. Paradoxically, while their early experiences, often humiliations, stay with them at the level of feeling and remembrance, these experiences have also contributed to the consciousness they have developed and the progressive careers they have chosen.

Cleaning Up the Trash

Fighting Shame

LINDA STOUT

I grew up very poor in the rural South. My father was a tenant farmer, and by the time I was five my mother had become completely disabled from a car wreck. I didn't really realize I was poor . . . at first. My parents were very loving, and I had a joyful life, working from the age of six, while at the same time being allowed to be a kid. I enjoyed my private time with my father when I got up an hour or two early to work in the fields before going to school. We didn't have a bathroom or running water, but I don't remember being dirty. My greatest joy was when we would have a warm summer rain and my mother would send us outside, naked with a bar of soap.

It was only when I started school that the differences began to show up. Another boy and I got made fun of a lot on the bus, especially by older kids. I never really understood why, but knew that the other boy was always dirty and felt that somehow that was the reason they lumped us together. I thought anyone who lived in a brick house, no matter how small and run-down, was rich. We lived the whole time I was growing up in a small ten-foot-by-forty-foot trailer parked on other people's land, so my dream was always to live in a house.

My other dream was to be a teacher. I started playing at being a teacher at the age of six with all my cousins and younger sisters. I would make a desk out of a cardboard box and then make them sit and listen to me teach. My mother told me I had to do really good at school if I wanted to become a teacher. And unlike many kids in my situation, my parents were able to make sure we stayed in school during harvest times.

I loved going to school and learning to read, so, at the beginning, I excelled. In first grade they moved me and five or six other students ahead to second grade. We were still considered first graders, but because we were able to read, they would combine us with the next grade up. I did that until I reached the third grade, sitting in a fourth-grade class. The teacher openly ridiculed some of the students, particularly those of us who were poor. She felt I was way too "uppity" for my position in life, and one day she brought me in front of the class to do long division. When I told her she had never showed us how to do long division and I couldn't do the problem, she mocked me in a singsong voice and told me I would never go to college or be a teacher. The other students joined her laughter. For many years I never told anyone what happened. I was so ashamed, and I began to believe that I could not be a good student. My grades went from A+ to average.

That same year, my best friend, Lou Jean, told me she wasn't allowed to come to my house, because her father said I was "white trash." I didn't understand what it meant, but I knew it was something to be ashamed of. I would spend hours obsessively making sure there was not one bit of trash anywhere around our house. Like for many people who lived in the country and in poverty, there was no such thing as trash pickup. We carried our trash out into a pile in the woods and burned what we could.

It wasn't until high school that my mother said to me, "If you want to go to college, you will have to make straight A's and get a scholarship." Luckily, my freshman year, I had a math teacher who believed in me and encouraged me to move out of the basic classes and into a college track. In order to get the credits I needed, I had to double up on many courses. The guidance counselor tried to tell me it was impossible and that I would not be allowed to do it. But between my math teacher, my mother, and my newfound determination, I persevered, graduating at the top of my class and getting a full scholarship into college.

After going to college for a year, I had to drop out because tuition went up $500 over what my scholarship covered. My father and I went to several storefront loan companies to try to get a loan, but because my parents didn't have $500 in collateral, we were unable to get the loan. I dropped out of college, moved into a trailer with several other women, and went to work in the textile mill.

I carried the shame of poverty with me throughout the next several years. I believed the messages that society gave me that if I was poor, somehow something must be wrong with me. I started hiding the fact I grew up poor and tried to pretend that I was "middle class." I began to live a lie that made me feel even worse about myself, and my self-esteem became even lower. I went on to become a secretary and eventually went to work for a civil rights attorney. It was a fit for me, having grown up Quaker, and I began to learn about civil rights and get involved in the women's and peace movements.

I suffered some of the worst classism in the progressive movement, because I, unlike most of the activists, did not have a broad base of knowledge about the world, did not have a college education, and, most of all, "talked funny" in my Appalachian southern dialect. It was not the usual kind of overt classism that I had experienced in school, and I now know it was not deliberate. But there was always an expectation that everyone in the group had gone to college. A common question was, "Where did you go to college?" or "What was your major?" I was too ashamed to answer that I had not gone to college and would give the name of the college that I briefly attended.

There was also an understanding that I was not privy to what a leader or trainer was. I knew I did not fit that definition because I didn't speak "right" or didn't know enough by the standards held up to us in the various organizing trainings I attended. I was discouraged from thinking I could become an organizer or a leader. When I mentioned wanting to apply for an organizing job in the national peace movement, even friends who were activists discouraged me, saying the movement was looking for specific kinds of skills (implying that I did not have those skills). When I volunteered to speak to a local group of ministers, I was told by a person in the group they felt another man who was a doctor would be more accepted as a speaker. When I went to workshops on organizing, I would leave feeling like even more of a failure, because I didn't fit the "ideal" of what a speaker or organizer was. The trainers used language and ways of being that were totally unfamiliar to me, and I began to believe that the peace movement was not for people like me.

In the end, I did become an organizer. Other southern organizers who worked with poor people recognized my passion and my skills, and believed in me. I still carried the shame of poverty and hid the fact I did not have a college education, and often would not admit to not knowing things that everyone else took for granted. For example, I remember once admitting in a local peace group that I did not know that the Japanese were held in internment camps in the United States in World War II. People were incredulous and laughed at me. They did not understand that I grew up where I was not taught these things—that my public high school substituted fundamentalist Bible class for U.S. history. So I learned to silence myself and not ask questions, pretending I knew things that I didn't.

I became a different person—a powerful person—when I was working with poor people. I realized that my voice had a place. I was successful in organizing in my home community—a community where many outside organizers had failed to make any headway. We began to win real victories and make real political change in our communities. I found that poor people really did care about peace and justice when it was talked about in a way they understood. I found my voice and my power, and yet I still felt the shame and powerlessness of poverty in settings outside my own community.

It was only when I went to Nicaragua that I saw people who lived in severe poverty with many similarities to the way I grew up, but who felt very differently about it. Talking with organizers in Nicaragua helped me understand poverty better, and my beliefs began to change. In Nicaragua, I met people who acknowledged poverty, but who were proud of who they were. They were revolutionaries who knew that the poverty they suffered was a problem of the system—not their personal fault. I came back from that trip with a determination to "come out of the closet" as a poor person.

As I began to talk about the experiences of growing up poor and trying to overcome my shame that somehow it was my fault, many other people would come up to me admitting they carried the same shame and secrecy. Together we worked to shift our consciousness and helped each other rid ourselves of the classism we had internalized.

The hardest part was that my mother could never handle me talking about growing up in poverty. She carried so much shame and guilt that when I would talk about it in front of her, she would say, "We tried to be good parents." I could never help her understand that it was not her fault. Nor was it the fault of my father, who worked all his life sixty or more hours a week. My mother died carrying her shame with her.

It took many years for me to overcome all the messages that society tells us about poor people—messages that become part of our own beliefs about ourselves. And, even now, sometimes one person's classist attitude can throw me back to that place of believing I'm not good enough, not smart enough, or not strong enough to be an organizer, an author, or a leader. And yet, I am all of those things, and some days I actually believe it about myself.

North American Peasant

FISHER LAVELL

"Mom?"

"Mm hm?"

"Why don't people like us?"

That was me, about twelve years old, sitting at the kitchen table coloring a picture of a bird-dog pup. And my mom over at the sink, doing some kind of work, maybe peeling potatoes or doing dishes or washing plastic bread bags to be hung on the clothesline and reused many times over. That was the 1960s, so we didn't have indoor plumbing, and she would have had to carry the water in pails from our neighbor's place a city block away. Of course, we weren't in the city but in a small prairie town in northern Manitoba, Canada.

"What do you mean, people don't like us? People don't *not* like us."

"Sure they do."

"Like who?"

"I don't know. Just people. People uptown. People at church."

"Well, people at church don't not like us. They like us. They love us, just like Jesus taught. Love everybody. You know that."

"Well, I don't feel that they love us. I don't feel that they like us. I feel that they don't like us."

"Well, I don't know why you'd say that. They like everybody at the church. They treat us the same as everybody else."

"Not really."

"Of course they do. We can go there, we can sit wherever we want, the pastor shakes your hand every Sunday! The ladies say good morning to you and me and everybody else."

"Yeah, I guess. But it's not the same. I don't know, it's just that they don't look at us the same. They sort of . . . hold back or something. Like they treat us nice because they're supposed to treat us nice. But it doesn't feel like they like us."

Little birds chirp and sing in the trees outside, and I point out lots of examples, which she explains away. I make lots of arguments, but she stands firm. About how nobody treats us different or dislikes us, not the people at church or the business people or the health providers or the kids at school.

"Yeah, I don't know. I don't know why. I just know that they don't like us, that's all, and they treat us different."

"Well, I don't know why you would say that. Sometimes, for a smart girl, you sure talk crazy. Why shouldn't people like us? We're just as good as anybody else."

I put a dark brown trim around the puppy's edges and am very pleased with the effect of the lighter brown on his body and floppy ears. "I know we are as good as anybody else, Mom. Everybody is as good as anybody else. I just feel that other people don't know we are. And they don't like us."

Years later, I would read in a university women's studies course about Betty Friedan's so-called "problem that has no name," the malaise of affluent, educated white women in the unsettling new world of baby-booming suburbia. But from the time I was very young, I struggled to identify and express what it was about me and my family that made us somehow different from other people—and treated differently.

This was a lonely task. Although I was wowing my family and teachers with my abilities and promise, among my large extended family I was a class of one. The smart one; the girl who was going somewhere. All around me, I could see the woman's life I never, ever wanted. Big-bellied at fourteen, quitting school to marry a drinking man who would beat them, fool around, sometimes even abuse the kids. And for all that I was on my way up and out, I loved my people.

I admired and adored my rugged old uncles, who always lost their legs to war or disease. My hard-drinking errant aunties, who loved to laugh and dance and party, often dying young. But that's not who I was going to be. I always balanced precariously on a stubborn ledge of refusal to distance myself from them, yet determination not to be how they were. Never under the wing of others; yet always different from my own.

Measured by money, education, and privilege, I lived in poverty. My parents both came from large, poor rural families and had never passed grade five. My father was, as my mother said, a jack-of-all-trades, and yet, unlike the saying, he was a master of all. He was a fine carpenter, could operate any kind of machine or vehicle, worked for the farmers as a laborer, slaughterer and meat cutter, and could track, hunt, and trap with the best of them. He was self-taught on guitar and a wonderful singer.

I grew up in a one-room house. There was a curtain that separated the bedroom from the living area. We had a woodstove, no electricity, no plumbing, no phone. My dad was sometimes employed, often traveling away to work the hydro or oil jobs. We rarely had cash money, and when Dad returned from somewhere with a big check, most of it paid down the debt at the grocery store.

My mom kept a big garden, also chickens, pigeons, and rabbits. And what we didn't eat fresh, she canned to last us till the next summer. When the meat ran out, my dad would walk down the tracks with his .22 and come back with partridge or prairie chicken. Or jump into a truck with a bunch of my uncles and return with venison. We never felt poor.

I was a very content child; the long grasses and bush paths were my playground, and my cousins and neighbors, my fun. It seemed wondrous to me when my mother told people that we lived in a little stand of poplars, just on the outskirts of town. As if our lives were a merry whirl and twirl of some great giant tree-lady's festive gown.

My mother and father walked very different paths. My mother was religious, her church the original loud, overzealous "Holy Rollers." My father's tithes and offerings went faithfully to the bar at the Valley Hotel. My mother stood alone in her religion, teasingly criticized for years, but she never wavered. She shared in the weddings, the ball games, card games, and house parties with her family and in-laws. But when it came to certain things, she neither judged nor participated. She lived the old saying I once found silly, "Hate the sin, love the sinner."

She never left my father. Not that he didn't deserve it, but because she had made a promise before God.

When I was a young child, my father's trips "uptown" seemed unproblematic and heralded his return in high spirits with trinkets and exotic cartons of Flamingo Café fish 'n' chips. But very soon the fun was rare, the troubles many. He did some terrible things. "Forgive and forget," I hear people say, but I'm more drawn to the Irish saying "Remember and forgive." How can we learn if we don't remember?

Although the years of my growing up wore the taint of my father's fall to drink, some of my fondest memories are of sitting up in the wee hours, with my dad on guitar singing the old songs. I believe in large part I developed the insights and abilities I use in my work today from the hours of sitting in the kitchen, singing Old Hank, Don Williams, and Roy Acuff; listening with my heart to my father's deep wounding.

Never expressed in his own words, but there in the songs, thick as blood. "Your Cheatin' Heart." "I Can't Stop Loving You." "Blue Eyes Crying in the Rain."

I graduated with honors and moved to the city—because I had to—for my education, for work. And as the Dixie Chicks put it, "to make my big mistakes."

In university psychology courses, I met up with theories that I should have applied. I read about people with low socioeconomic status and low self-esteem, addicted, sexually victimized, suffering from learned helplessness. I knew those people, but I was not one of them.

I owed this to my father, a proud and self-reliant man who wouldn't take welfare no matter how much we did without. I owed this to my mother, who refused to collude in my father's addiction. My course notes told me that the alcoholic had a dysfunctional wife, the codependent, whose behaviors complemented and enabled his addiction. But although my father had been the former, my mother was never the latter. She refused to placate, coddle, or absolve. Our home had often been a place of loud arguments, but my tenacious mother's children were safe, nourished, and never neglected.

My own journey to understanding the meaning of social class has meandered through varied terrain. I was introduced to the concept in a course on the history of social control, led by a self-proclaimed socialist professor. I was keenly involved with the course and got A's on my papers, but was shocked at my "zero points for participation." This was based on the three classes that I had missed because of sick-child issues. The prof stated disdainfully that my day-care problems were not her concern. "It is simply unprofessional," she said. "People who can't be responsible should not choose to become parents."

During those years, my father's many health problems culminated in the amputation of his leg. There were many worries and struggles. And though I was raising children and financing my degree on student loans, I remember accepting my mother's collect phone calls and wiring her a bus ticket to come stay with me. Quite a reversal of the "typical" student scenario.

I also remember my teenage nephew asking me for an expensive gift. When I said I couldn't do it and suggested that he ask his mother, he said, "No way would she buy me that. All her money goes to smokes and partying. And anyway, she said to ask you because you're rich." I sat him down and showed him the math; that on welfare his mother was getting more money than I was on student loans, and I had to pay my tuition off the top and then repay what I had borrowed.

We live in a society that validates victimhood, and nobody apologizes for weakness anymore. In my extended family today, there is a perception that people who don't glory in dysfunction are powerful and lucky and somehow owe those who do. Money, time, help unending. In all these, I have been unstintingly generous. Yet I can't help but notice that this is a one-way arrangement. While I owe them, they owe me nothing; not appreciation, not support or even respect. Their hand is always out, and I am expected to pay, pay, pay.

Professionals too mistake me for a member of the privileged class; based on skin color, I guess. When I was doing my master's degree, a white professor questioned the presence of an aboriginal woman in my qualitative research study. I said that the woman was poor, and my study was specifically from a working-class perspective.

But what qualifications did I have to interview a woman of color? I began by mentioning some Native Studies coursework, and she said, "Well all right then, as long as you're informed."

I sat quietly, head cocked, trying to figure out her logic. To me, the authority of my analysis—if intelligent and perceptive thought held no sway—came from the fact that I was raised in a family and neighborhood in which white skin was just one of many shades.

In 1907 Ontario, my Irish immigrant grandmother married a black man, the son of a liberated slave who came up on the Underground

Railroad. They had two surviving children, and when her husband was killed in World War I, she married my dad's father, a Canadian Frenchman, and they had seven children. Two of my dad's sisters, as well as two of my mom's brothers, married Canadian aboriginal women, and they all had big families.

Of the twenty families living on the outskirts with us, there were very few who had solely European ancestry. The community celebrations of my childhood were luscious with Métis fiddlers, country guitars, and an old cowboy named McCoy playing the spoons; waltzes, polkas, and Irish jigs; pierogies and garlic sausage; bannock, rabbit stew, and blueberry pie.

It is just not true that all white people have the privilege of dominance, or a history as conquerors. My genealogical research confirmed that every branch of my family tree came from poverty. A far-flung relation, Dr. Agnes Groome, did up a book on our forebears. She noted in the introduction that, of the seven thousand persons studied, not one was part of any group with wealth or decision-making power.

Culture—the sum total of how we live—is not the same thing as skin color or racial identity. And culture is relevant to everything. I remember, in a feminist research course, extensively critiquing the literature on motherhood, using particularly the writing of black and working-class theorists. Though I thoroughly showed feminist theory's base in the experiences of affluent-class white women, they heard me wrong. I was harangued and jeered for my alleged "anti-choice stance."

But I made the sacrifices that had to be made to pay my own way and to raise my children in a middle-class area, a "better" area, away from the chaos and danger of downtown. And my children indeed did not get drawn into the gang violence, drug lifestyles, or sex trades that my other young relatives did. But my own children were essentially raised middle class in a white community.

In many ways, I was the only politicizing influence in my children's lives—a heavy burden for a woman alone in a context that respected neither her class nor her gender. My children were sometimes influenced by the dominant values and sexist mores around them, sometimes irked by their difficult mother, who failed to apologize in advance for what she was about to say, and neither manipulated nor deferred as "niceness" required.

It has been years now that I have been thinking about this concept of class and what makes us different. And while I know that my parents' low income was important to how I am today as a person, I also think that many of the strengths of my background are unique to its rural setting. In a small town, they can still hold you in low regard, but they cannot easily separate you out for punishment with inferior schools, ugly surroundings, and greater crime.

For myself, I have begun to describe the kind of people I came from as North American peasants. To some extent, in spite of several so-called revolutions in between, our people still come closest to possessing the knowledge base and the skills that once gave relative self-sufficiency to the common people. And nature, the land, is still there. That Great Dancing Lady—like the giant tree lady of my childhood—is immensely forgiving, and for those who put themselves in her hands, become her pupils, She still sustains.

Survivorship is a gift of my poverty-class upbringing. Resiliency, the ability to take the blows and come up swinging. Empathy, generosity, an open heart; things you acquire from being rejected, doing without, and carrying a burden alone.

I have the gift of story because stories were how we colored our lives in. Every uncle and aunt and neighbor was immortalized in story. Raggedy they were, but heroes nonetheless. I love to sing; I possess the ability to be totally, boisterously right here, right now. As Steinbeck put it, "We are the people that live."

The limitations of my background are mainly in the staggering effect of the hidden privileges whose lack our lives feel so keenly. With great sacrifice and commitment, I have been able to pay my own way and raise my children well. But I have no savings, and my children start at zero—not behind and at risk, but they too must pay for themselves. Like me, they live in a world that presumes, based on their skin color, that they possess a wealth of psychological, social, and financial resources. But they don't, and so they struggle.

Today, I have an education and a great job. My current family still deals with frustrations and disappointments, bias and unpleasantness, systems and people with power who just do not seem to like us. But we just shake our heads and say, "Must be a class issue. And we must be working class." Those are the words we have finally found to explain the problem that used to have no name.

I Work with Worn-Out Tools

JANET LIGHTFOOT

I was born into the culture of hunger and had parents who were unable to pay the rent. I recall the Good Humor man often giving me free ice cream that would be my nourishment for the day. I call it a culture of hunger because I cried myself to sleep, due to the body-wrenching hunger pangs—the kind where the front of the belly reaches for the back and nothing interferes with the trip.

Today I am remembered as the woman who helps poor people with their applications for town welfare. I'm also known as the woman who speaks out about official abuse. I speak of it so often that everyone gets frustrated when my mouth opens. That would be the government officials who misquote laws to turn away people who are really eligible.

When I was young my mother would go without eating so my two younger sisters and I could eat. She also made sure I finished whatever was before me. If I didn't like the lamb stew, it was reheated and waiting for me the next day. "Waste not!" was the motto. I learned to leave food for my younger sisters, even when I was still hungry. Poverty is not a black thing; it discriminates equally against all races.

When my baby brother lived only three hours, my mother had me stay with one of her friends. They treated me better than my parents did. I decided I was adopted, looked everywhere for my real birth certificate, but couldn't find it. I would love to tell you that I grew up in a wonderful loving family—only it ain't so. Neither of my parents was treated kindly as a kid. So they lacked the love skills.

When I was in second grade, I asked Mary Anne, the next-door neighbor kid, to come out and play with me. But her parents wouldn't let her. They had heard me yell out in pain when my father jumped on my belly because I left a dirty dress in the wrong place. They thought I must have been a bad kid to make my parents beat me.

When Kennedy was president, I remembered the federal government coming up with a mathematical formula to decide who's poor. Molly Orshansky expected her formula to be modified as time went on. It was based on the cost of food. I told my parents that the formula should include all of life's basic needs. They told me I was just a kid and didn't know what I was talking about. And any job was better than none, even jobs that paid only half of what people needed for rent, food, and repairs. I didn't get hit that time. I knew enough to be quiet, no matter what I believed.

Today I tell my wonderful partner that having a job pay $10 an hour when it costs at least $17.50 to live on is not a good paying job. I'm tired of all that "any job is better than no job" talk. My partner feels bad, threatened when my opinion is different from hers. Maybe I challenge the belief system that her parents gave her. I became an advocate for the poor and homeless. As a kid when the rent became due we were homeless, at least for a while. I thought everyone had the right to have a home. I joined a spiritual group, and was taken into other people's homes for as long as they could stand me, couch-surfing for a month at a time. Finally I was placed with a pastor's family. Then an agency helped me find a very small two-room apartment. Someone gave me dishes and a can opener. That was great. Then when I moved to a three-room apartment, people couch-surfed on my bed or on the floor.

Later, a group of us wanted to help those in need. The focus was on all people. Not just families, or alcoholics, or even people with a mental diagnosis, or battered women, but everyone, both the rich and the poor. We restored a vacant house and opened a transitional shelter. The first two who came to the shelter were a lesbian couple. One was good at office things, and the other good at changing beds and making meals. They stayed on as staff. We were good listeners and involved the people who stayed with us in our plans and decisions. But we couldn't pay the bills and were thousands of dollars in arrears. Finally, when the government withdrew its support because it didn't like my sexual orientation, we had to close the shelter. One guy who had nowhere else to go slept on the couch in my apartment for the next four years.

Now, my focus is still on trying to help poor people, but I use my telephone and whatever people skills I have. I tell people who expect to be homeless to fight the eviction. I tell them the steps to follow and to call Legal Aid. Calling Legal Aid can often be another hit-or-miss farce. At one point there were six or seven Legal Aid lawyers for 125,000 people. But people who could afford a lawyer are in a system with 400 persons per lawyer.

I also told families and individuals what General Assistance was supposed to do. And I told my clients how to appeal a bad decision. If GA worked according to state law, I would not need to be calling up the top GA person with the state. I would not need to call churches, which last year gave a limited amount of funds for the poor. And it all went for heating, not housing.

Each time a city or town in Maine rewrites General Assistance laws and turns someone away who is eligible, my job gets harder. I try all kinds of approaches to rectify this. I got a lobbying group together to sponsor a state bill placing signs quoting the actual eligibility laws as they were passed—not how they were twisted. I sued the state when they still turned away folks who did qualify for aid. But they said I lacked "standing," like it was a violation of my right to help others.

When Mom had a stroke in 2003, it left nearly all of her left side paralyzed. I took her in and cared for her for over three years. I did not force her to eat three-day-old food. That was a gift I gave not just to her, but to myself.

I wonder if Mr. Obama will be in favor of the correct things to end poverty. Or will he merely place another Band-Aid on 15 percent to 30 percent of the people? I want to work myself out of a nonpaying job, to where everyone earns or receives government benefits in the amount required to take care of all basic needs. I want to work toward a land where all are fed and all have a bed, dignity, and rights. I work with worn-out tools.

Mexican Girl from Fontana

GENEVA REYNAGA-ABIKO

The personal experience of being a successful Mexican American female who is originally from a lower social class background is very powerful for me. Interwoven throughout my journey is a continued awareness that I am very fortunate, that hard work is essential but not sufficient for prosperity, and that I must never forget where I come from if I hope to help others like me succeed. As one of the few Latinas in a field (psychology) that is over 95 percent European American, I have struggled with a lack of mentors available to guide me throughout my educational journey. I am interested in sharing my story with the hope of inspiring change in others by challenging common assumptions and stereotypes.

To start at the beginning of my own consciousness and sense of place, I should explain that my grandparents immigrated to the United States from Mexico in the 1940s. They walked to Arizona from Sonora, Mexico, and found work on ranches. My grandparents had very little formal schooling in Mexico (less than three years of elementary school) and could not read or write in Spanish. However, they very quickly learned how to speak English. Eventually they became literate in both English and Spanish, something I continue to find amazing and inspiring.

A short time later, my grandfather somehow learned of job opportunities at a steel mill in Fontana, California. Mr. Kaiser, of Kaiser Steel as it was known back then, was hiring workers to keep up with demand created by World War II. He promised "papers" (that is, legal citizenship) and health insurance at his local hospital (Kaiser Hospital) for all his employees. My grandfather secured a position, bought a house that people in the United States would characterize as tiny, and worked at the steel mill until he retired at age seventy-two. My family has lived in Fontana ever since, and the next three generations were born at Kaiser Hospital.

I grew up with a keen awareness of my ethnicity as a Mexican American from an immigrant family but had no idea about class. I was raised by my mother and her family, shopping at outdoor "swap meets" and secondhand stores. We were called "rich" by my extended family in Mexico. I felt fortunate that we always had enough food and clothes, with a few brand names thrown into the mix when we were lucky enough to find them for less than a dollar. I had no idea that the food we were getting was left over from what others did not want to eat or that we could be considered poor for eating beans, rice, and homemade tortillas every day.

When I was ten years old, my mother decided to move my sister and me to a small town on the East Coast, away from our family and everything we knew. She and her husband (my stepfather) had found a very inexpensive home in a town with so little crime there was not even a full-time police officer. I was traumatized to be so far away from my loved ones, particularly since we were the only non-white family in the town. I had no way of understanding my mother's desire to move away from high crime rates and poor schools. The public school in our new town was far better than anything in Fontana, and I was able to get a private-school-quality education for free.

I first started noticing class when we moved to this small town. People accused me, in no uncertain terms, of being "rich" because I was from California. They saw my "city clothes" and heard my accent and were convinced I was from a place where movie stars walked around all day and everyone went to the beach to get a tan. The part of California I was from was not represented on television and so did not exist for these children. I was confused by their treatment of me and retreated to my books and journals until graduating from high school with a 4.0 grade-point average.

I was the first person in my large, extended family to go to college. My mother and a few of her siblings were awarded scholarships in music but could not go to college because they needed to stay home and work to help the family survive financially. One of my younger cousins graduated from a local state university, and a few other cousins went to a community college for a short time, but none of them were very academically successful. Did their poor schools with large class sizes and lack of textbooks have anything to do with the difference in our educational success?

Class differences were very apparent to me in college. I returned to California for school and was shocked at the nice cars I saw in the parking lots. I never dreamt that a young person could drive a car that costs more money than my entire family makes in one year. I had no idea that there were students who did not have to work while going to school. I could not imagine having parents who paid for full tuition and all associated expenses. I was dismayed to see so many students getting bad grades and wasting time changing majors and failing classes. It was such an honor for me to be in college that I could not understand why others seemed to take it for granted. While I noticed these class differences, I did not challenge my own background and continued to feel a close part of my family.

Very quickly after graduating college, I started to feel like my family treated me differently. They did not understand why I needed to continue my education and assumed I would be "rich" because I was a college graduate. It was in graduate school that I began to understand that my class background was somewhere between that of my family of origin and that of my peers. In one of my first master's level courses, I remember a classmate laughing at my accent. He was asking me why I "talked like that," laughing at my "ghetto accent," and I felt both confused and embarrassed because he was Latino and I expected him to come from the same background as I did.

Around the same time, I became good friends with someone from a different ethnicity and class background. He was from a country where only the very rich can afford to immigrate to the United States. He often pointed out that my choice of words and way of speaking socially located me as "lower class." In his opinion, I was "too smart" to talk like that and needed to change if I was going to be a doctor. At the time I found this highly offensive and confusing. My family had always told me that appearances did not matter and that as long as I was smart enough, I could do anything. My friend's advice, however, proved to be very helpful throughout my development as a psychologist.

As a doctoral student, I very much struggled with class. I often describe my doctoral education as training in "class socialization" because I felt like the program was trying to make me into someone who was comfortable charging a lot of money for services and who spoke and dressed "like a doctor," whatever that means. My professors never said anything overt to give me this impression, but doctoral training was the first time I felt like I had to start separating from my family if I was going to fully understand and succeed in the profession I had chosen.

I remain the only person in my family to attend graduate school and obtain a doctorate. While they are proud of me, my family members accuse me of "being white" for moving away from home and living in a neighborhood they could never afford. They do not understand how far from true this is or how much it hurts me, especially because I have centered my career on addressing diversity issues and giving back to communities in need.

I often feel guilty for not returning to Fontana, where much of my family still lives. It is an interesting struggle, though, because I am positive that my grandparents came to the United States so many decades ago to have a better life. While they never stressed education per se, my grandfather was very proud to see me obtain a doctorate shortly before he passed away. I am confident that, even though my family overtly criticize me for being so different from them, they are unconsciously happy that I have been able to leave the crime-ridden city where we were all born. While they do not understand what I do for a living or the idea that one can be called "doctor" without working in a medical setting, I am sure they are proud of me.

My family remains a large influence on my life and career path. I am grateful to them for teaching me hard work, the value of not complaining when times are tough, and the importance of sticking together as a family and helping each other in whatever way we can. I am grateful for how lucky we all are to live in a country with the opportunity to make a livable wage. I find that these values make me very different from many of my colleagues, whom I sometimes feel do not appreciate what they have or expect things to always go well. The politics of higher education have been easier for me to survive because of my values, although it has been difficult to find mentors from similar ethnic and class backgrounds. I wish my family could understand that, far from "being white," I identify very strongly as a Mexican American and try to represent my ethnicity well wherever I go and in everything I do.

I have learned quite a few things throughout my journey. Education has been key to my success, and I cannot imagine a better way to move up the social class ladder than through obtaining advanced degrees. I am fortunate to have a pristine academic background. However, I have suffered from classism and racism throughout this journey and rarely see others in the academy who look like me, even though I completed my degrees in a region that has one of the highest Latino populations in the United States. I also continue to struggle with student loan debt that many of my colleagues do not have. I do not regret this, because I could not have completed my education otherwise, but it poses certain struggles that those from higher class backgrounds do not face.

Another struggle I have faced is lack of guidance and mentorship. I have never had a professor who represented my sociocultural background, with regard to ethnicity or class. It is important to find sources of support that can elucidate the norms for higher classes, especially since families of origin may not understand the difference in values. It has taken me many years to fully grasp the importance of developing one's image, but I have learned how incorrect my family members were in their advice that such things did not matter. While I wish I lived in a world where their words were true, I recognize that I am very much judged by how I speak, wear my hair, dress, what jewelry I choose to wear, how I do my makeup, etc. This frustrates me at times, but I recognize the importance of "looking like a doctor" if I expect to be treated like one.

I have also found that ethnicity and class intersect in very interesting ways. It is difficult to separate them for me; I am certain that my life would have been different if I came from a higher class background, or if I was poor but not Mexican American. My family background supports the stereotype of "poor Mexicans," but my current class stand-ing does not. I have found that it is very difficult for people to under-stand this. For example, in the neighborhood where I now live I am regularly stared at for being nonwhite. At the same time, I am stared at by those in my hometown whenever I visit, because I no longer fit the class assumptions of that social location. It seems difficult to find a place where I can be accepted as an educated, successful Latina.

I understand how fortunate I am to be where I am today. I have finally found a small network of professionals who are more like me, and we provide support to each other through e-mail and contact at professional conferences. No matter where I find a job, it is always true that I am quite different from my peers in the languages I speak, the music I listen to, the food I eat, and other behaviors that socially locate me. While I am finally able to "speak the language" that is expected of me in my role as a professional, I still feel like a Mexican American girl from Fontana deep down inside. I wish I could inte-grate each aspect of my identity into a unified whole, but I am not confident that higher education as it currently exists would welcome all of my social background.

In a deliberate effort to help others break the cycle of what is socially expected of them, I mentor students and young professionals whenever I can and share my story in ways that are supportive of strug-gle. I have always felt the importance of giving back to historically disadvantaged groups. I think a part of me feels like an outlier for "making it," and I give all I can so that others may not have to struggle in the ways I did. I want our future leaders to know that they are not the "only ones," and that it is okay to be different from where they come from, even if their families of origin do not understand. It is okay to be from a "low class" background even when one's current peers assume negative things about "those people." We need to learn how to speak the language of success as it currently exists, but in doing so, we must remember who we are and where we come from to slowly change the stereotype of what success looks like. Our historic ability to work hard and survive without the privileges of the dominant group can certainly push us through!

What They Say about Poor Girls

STEPHANIE JONES

I know what they say about poor girls.

Tryin' to get pregnant to keep a boy around.

Havin' babies to get a welfare check.

Trappin' men by tellin' 'em they're on the pill when they're not.

Hell, I was even in a hospital not too long ago when a receptionist started talkin' about the poor girls around town who were taught by their parents to have "no morals" and to start pumpin' out those babies as soon as possible to get more money comin' in.

Of course that woman didn't know she was talkin' to a poor girl inside the woman's body who had health insurance and classy lookin' clothes on. She assumed I was like her—middle class or whatever— and hatin' on folks without insurance or with Medicaid or looking for some kind of supposed free ride.

But you know what assumptions do, and they did it right there in the hospital when I was fumin' mad about what she was sayin' and she just kept on sayin' it. Even followed me out to the waiting room to tell me she was raisin' her girl different. She was the ass because she wouldn't shut her mouth and didn't know what she was talking about, and I was the ass because I was the very kind of girl she *was* talking about.

Even though she didn't know what she was talking about.

I don't even recognize what people say about poor girls though.

Trying to get pregnant?

All my life I've been with girls and women doing everything they could to *avoid* pregnancy. Well, almost everything, since most of them still had sex. So, I'll put it this way—the girls and women I knew who were having sex were doing everything they could to not get pregnant. And they talked about it all the time.

This pill.

That pill.

This condom.

That condom.

Pull out.

Watch the calendar.

Count days from your period.

Know your options if it happens.

Let me be clear here. The girls and women in my family think kids are just as adorable as the next person does. We just knew the costs.

Mostly we knew about financial costs like being out of work because you're sick while you're pregnant then being out of work because you're in the hospital having the baby then being out of work because you're recovering then being out of work because your kid is sick then being out of work because the babysitter didn't show up then being out of work because you're just too damn exhausted to get your ass out of bed on time to go to work.

One day off work could mean the light bill isn't paid.

Two days could mean rent is short.

Three days? Don't even go there.

We knew the financial costs because every woman we knew suffered those. We didn't know anyone who was salaried or got paid personal days, paid maternity leave, paid vacation.

We didn't know a woman who didn't worry too much about going in an hour or so late when a kid was sick.

We only knew women who clocked in and clocked out and were only paid for the work their bodies did during the minutes between those two times.

We only knew women who busted their asses on the restaurant floor, behind a bar, on the factory line, cleaning someone else's house, over the café grill, watching someone else's kids, poking cash register keys, dry-cleaning clothes.

We watched our women come home off the bus, out of a friend's car, out of a relative's car, out of a borrowed car, out of a barely-gonna-make-it-but-it's-my-own car, and they were tired.

Pooped.

Exhausted. And they knew and we knew that *still* when the check came in or the tips were added up it wasn't going to quite cover what it needed to cover.

It wasn't gonna cover the grocery bill after all the bills were paid, it wasn't gonna cover the field trip money expected at school, it wasn't gonna cover the new shoes little Sammy needed after his toes burst out the front, it wasn't gonna cover the drive-in movie she promised the kids on the weekend, it wasn't gonna cover bus fare or gas or the small payment she gave to her friend who drove every day.

It never quite covered.

Something was always left uncovered.

Exposed.

Poor girls are exposed all the time to the harsh and judging world, and their exposures are spat out of people's mouths, "Look at her, now why on earth would you dress like that?" "What's she doing with a boy that age? She's just *trying* to be like her welfare queen mama." "Don't even think about dating her. She's a gold digger if I've ever seen one."

You've heard more of this spewing than me of course, because most of the time I was excluded company when these things were being said.

But my world of you-better-not-get-pregnant-girl and dear-god-it's-me-poor-girl-please-don't-let-me-get-pregnant and oh-my-god-what-am-I-gonna-do-now weebled from side to side when I realized that some girls tried to get pregnant.

Rich girls though.

And I'd never heard you-know-those-rich-girls-only-tryin'-to-get-pregnant one time ever in my life. Never.

And girls that weren't so rich, but had more money than I'd ever known, were doing it too.

Yep. I was stunned when I found out that those girls I never knew tried to get pregnant.

Shocked I'm tellin' ya.

Shakin' my head and blowin' through my nose I tried to get a handle on this new world I was discovering.

Not only did some girls (or women, by the time I knew them) plan to get pregnant, they made it a full-time job to figure out how to get pregnant.

Damn.

They should just talk to some of the girls I knew who seemed to know the secret even when they were tryin' everything to avoid it.

But these girls are se-ri-ous. Fertility books, visits to the doctor, prenatal vitamins months before they even thought they would try to conceive, halting their alcohol habits, curbing their caffeine intakes, thermometers, sex on certain days, calling in their spouses when the temperature was just right, doing all kinds of yoga positions immediately following sex, reading more books, seeing more doctors, getting shots, paying thousands and thousands of dollars to try to get pregnant.

I mean damn. Again.

This world was so foreign to me.

"You mean you do all this to *get* pregnant?"

And they think the poor girls are tryin' to get pregnant.

But poor girls are so strapped by their finances we can't imagine a pregnancy, the furniture needed, time away from work, the long-term financial costs, the exhaustion after a double shift, the food, the bottles, the formula, the child care.

Other girls, to my amazement, seem to have the pleasure and luxury of focusing on the "joy" of pregnancy, the "joy" of nursing, the "joy" of child-rearing, the "joy" of becoming a mother who has the time and resources to make a room for the newcomer, to buy all the necessities (plus) for the baby, to take time off work to recuperate, to visit the doctor without worrying about the bills, to take the baby to a pediatrician who works in a colorful, spacious, inviting office in the suburbs rather than wait in long lines at the cold, damp, gray, local health clinic to see the one pediatrician who comes each month.

I know what they say about poor girls.

But I think they got it wrong.

I'm thirty-seven years old now, and after giving birth to an unplanned beautiful baby girl who is now seven years old and the love of my life, I'm still trying to avoid pregnancy.

It's in me.

The fear.

The anxiety.

I have insurance now.

A salary.

Time off when I need it.

And the room for a new baby in the family.

But I know the costs.

And I still feel exposed.

Better Than

PATIENCE RAGE

I knew she was better than me because of all the things she had and the ways she was cared for by her family.

We were in the fourth grade at Stokely School in the Strawberry Mansion section of North Philadelphia. She sat to the left of me, three rows from the front. I always felt dirty sitting next to her. And I didn't think or know why.

You could tell her mother combed, brushed, and plaited her hair every morning before school. Her face was always shiny and clean. She smiled a lot and smelled good, like baby oil. At no time were her knees ever ashy.

She was better than me because she wore pleated skirts all the time, with clean white blouses with pressed round collars. A gold necklace with a tiny cross hung over her buttoned blouse. Her socks were always clean and folded down evenly around her ankles, just before the straps of her patent-leather shoes.

When it rained she wore a raincoat, a rain scarf that snapped closed at the strings, and rain boots that slipped on with her shoes. That was boss.

When she opened her notebook it was neat and clean. She had a plaid book-bag, a loose-leaf book, and a black-and-white composition book. There were no jelly stains on her homework. A plastic thing that snapped right into her loose-leaf book held all her sharpened pencils and never-even-used erasers and a key ring with a single key that read "welcome home."

We laughed a lot, and never one time from her was I made to feel she was better than me. I just knew it.

My friend lived in a house with just her mother and father.

I was pretty unkempt as a little girl. I have few memories of my mother reluctantly straightening my hair and burning the tips of my ears always because she was hurried to move on to the next task at hand.

What I now know to be chaos is what my family looked like most times. I had an auntie that could do hair well, but she had her own ways. We were living at this time with my grandmother and grandfather again because Momma and Booker T. had another fight. Adults can be so boring.

My grandparents owned a three-story house on a tree-lined block in Strawberry Mansion. Every morning, I had to look for my homework book. One time I found it under the bed. There were four bedrooms in my grandparents' home. Momma and all of us kids stayed on the third floor front room. There were just six of us then.

I slept in a chair that pushed back and turned into a bed. It was really a lounge chair. My two brothers slept on a pallet. There was a crib that one of the two babies slept in. Momma had a bed that her knee baby and my youngest sister slept in with her. There was no room to walk. We stepped over and on each other all the time, especially through the night going to the bathroom. Sometimes we had to stay in the room because everyone was mad at Momma for some reason. No one said anything, but I could just tell that my brothers and sisters were treated different from other kids in the house.

My aunt Mildred stayed in the back room on the third floor. She's the one that can do hair real good. She's also the auntie that's always telling us to "be quiet" in our room. She and her husband got into a fight at their wedding, so now she lives in Grandmomma and Grandpapa's house, too. She's mean. I love her anyway. After every single day of work she comes home, says "Good evening," eats dinner, and goes to the "31" bar around the corner and doesn't come home until we are all in bed. I know because I'd hear her tiptoe up the steps, and that's when I could peacefully fall asleep. I was awakened every few hours by the hiss of the radiator.

Anyway, my aunt Mildred works six days a week sorting laundry at the hospital where I was born. She tells me I was born in this same hospital, and so was this famous blues singer named Billie Holiday. We were both born at Philadelphia General Hospital, also known as PGH. She tells me what this means. It means you could grow up and become a famous blues singer too. I believed her. She always told me the truth. Her truth. She loved her job and thought it was better than my mother's job. Said she'd kill herself before she'd clean behind some Jews.

My mom says she'd let her children starve to death before she'd shake the shit out of some sheets a bunch of old sick white folks wallowed in.

My grandmother and grandfather's bedroom is the second-floor front. They go to bed real early, so we always had to be quiet. Our room was directly over the top of them, and looks like no matter how quiet we were, we could never be quite as quiet as my grandparents needed us to be.

Papa gets up around four in the morning, and Grandmom gets up with him and makes breakfast; they have coffee, biscuits, and syrup together. Papa gets up, goes out, cranks his bus up, revs the engine, and in a few moments I realize it's the start of another day.

My grandfather has a school bus with his name on the side and some other writing I don't understand. He takes a load of people to Chatsworth, New Jersey, to pick blueberries. The house feels safe and warm. Back to sleep I go before the chaos starts.

My aunt Sister, her husband Willie, and their three children stay in the second-floor back room. They been there since they married. My momma says the youngest daughter always stays close to her momma. And Momma says they must have a ton of money because she can't see what they spend it on.

My uncle Willie drives for PTC (Philadelphia Transportation Company), and my auntie is a police officer. They are better than anyone in the house except my grandmother and grandfather. Like, secretly, they really are better than my grandmother and my grandfather because I hear them say what Momma and Papa should do, or what Momma and Papa could do.

Come to think of it, they really are better than us too. My auntie and uncle have a car, and they have a color television in their room.

Their children don't go to the same school as us. All of them have really nice clothes. My auntie separates their food from my mother's in the refrigerator. They have orange juice for breakfast. They eat food that's better than ours. Like if we have hot dogs and beans, well, I did the cooking a lot for my brothers and sisters. I cooked Mondays, Wednesdays, and Fridays, and I always treated us to hot dogs and beans and Kool-Aid on Fridays. My cousins would have smoky links, french fries, and apple juice.

Sometimes my momma got a chance to do one of our heads before she goes to work. She and my grandmother clean houses for two friends, Mrs. Cohen and Mrs. Weinberg. They live two doors away from each other in Oreland, Pennsylvania, and that's where my mother and grandmother traveled to every Monday, Wednesday, and Friday to clean their houses. On Tuesdays and Thursdays and some Saturdays Momma cleaned for an English professor who lived in the Alden Apartments in Germantown.

When I was around ten years old, one of the Weinberg girls got a pony for her birthday. I always wanted a pony. I loved ponies, too. When the man came through our street selling pony rides for a dime, up and down the street all day long, I never got a ride.

I thought about Joan Weinberg's pony like it was mine. I saw myself riding it. Joan and I would take turns riding. So, I asked my mother if I could go to work with her one day. It took a while, but somehow it worked out one day that I got to go with her. Not only did I not ride the pony, I never even got to see it. I imagined it would be in the backyard. I didn't know about stables. What I did get a chance to do was help Momma clean that house.

That was the biggest dream my mother could have for me was to teach me how to clean. For two reasons, she'd say; one is I'd know "how to" once I was married, and the other reason was I'd have to work somewhere someday. May as well start now.

Because we were not raised to think about college, I missed an opportunity. I was a good student at Thomas Shallcross Boarding School in Northeast Philadelphia and the school's first music student in 1968. I was awarded a scholarship to the University of Detroit; it required my mother coming to the school to sign some papers, which she never did.

I didn't hear the word "class" until I was in the tenth grade. I stepped out of line at school and shouted out to my housemother that I had to pee. Ms. Cornwall walked over to me and whispered, "You have no class, and the reason being, a young lady does not talk like that. Diane here has class"—she gestured with her head at my friend standing right next to me. I thought to myself, Diane also has a belly filled with baby. I don't have that either. I might be okay.

No Yellow Tickets

The Stigma of Poverty in the School Lunch Line

WENDY WILLIAMS

I never remember being denied anything that I wanted as a child—Barbies, Cabbage Patch dolls, Easy-Bake ovens—I had it all. Birthdays and Christmas were happy and lavish. We lived in suburban Virginia in a four-bedroom, two-bath, three-story colonial house with a large yard. My father commuted every day into Washington, D.C., to work for the government, while my mother stayed home to care for me and my two siblings.

My father had an affair, and my parents separated when I was in fifth grade. Although the outside of our home had not changed, every time I walked into the house I was aware of what was missing. Empty spaces where furniture used to be were a tangible reminder of both the fact that my father had left and that we couldn't afford to replace the lost furniture. Moreover, my mother wasn't there as much either because she had to get a job to help support us. Not only did I grieve that my family would no longer be whole, but I became painfully aware of my loss of freedom as well, since I was now the primary after-school babysitter for my younger handicapped sister.

Two years after my father left, my mother remarried and we moved to Knoxville, Tennessee. Although our new house was significantly smaller than our house in Virginia, we were still in a middle-class neighborhood, and I attended a well-regarded public high school. But our slide down the economic ladder was only stalled, not stopped.

When I was a sophomore, my stepfather lost his job and could not find work. This time our decline was swift. Before my mom and stepfather filed for bankruptcy, they took what capital they had and bought a small piece of land in the country, just outside the Great Smoky Mountains National Park. They plotted the design of the house on graph paper, and my stepfather and a friend built the house. I now had to share a bedroom with my younger sister.

That summer, instead of hanging out with my friends, I spent my time working on the house. I hammered nails, stapled insulation, and laid pipe for our water line, but I didn't do it willingly. Much of the time I was angry and sullen. I raged against what was happening to me. It wasn't fair. This isn't who I was. My parents scolded me for my attitude, and I yelled back with my anger at them for not protecting me. I didn't understand how they could let this happen.

As soon as the house was up to code, we moved in. Although the house was technically deemed "livable," nothing was finished; there was only unpainted drywall on the walls and subflooring on the floors. It remained that way until well after I left for college two years later.

Once we started having economic troubles and I stopped getting an allowance, I worked at a series of small, after-school jobs to buy the things I wanted. I cleaned offices, babysat, and worked at a fast-food restaurant. I was no longer the same social class as my friends, but many never knew.

Although we now lived in a different county that was more than an hour away from my middle-class high school, I lobbied my parents to allow me to commute there (illegally) every day for class. I used any excuse to get out of having friends come over to visit my new house. I was desperately afraid they wouldn't like me anymore if they saw how we were living. In addition, I spent a large chunk of my paychecks on clothing, favoring items that could be easily recognized as the "popular" labels of the time. I religiously shopped sales and traveled to the local outlet mall looking for name-brand clothing at cheaper prices. When I bought expensive clothing, I hid the bags from my parents and made sure they didn't see the clothes when I did my laundry. I was devastated one day when I wore my new (expensive) cream sweater and a boy bumped into me with his cheese nachos, staining the front of the sweater with orange goo. I was late to my next class because I stayed so long in the bathroom scrubbing the sweater to clean it and wiping the tears from my face because I knew it was ruined.

I was working incredibly hard to keep up appearances; however, the year my family filed for bankruptcy, my mother completed the paperwork for the free/reduced-price school lunch program. When my mother told me we qualified for the program, I yelled at her. "Are you kidding me? Why did you do that?" She was perplexed. "But Wendy, now you won't have to spend your money on lunch. You can use it for other things. This will help us." I couldn't believe she was so naive; she was undoing all my hard work. I was adamant, "No it won't because I am *not* using it."

What my mom didn't know was that all I could think about was my elementary school friend, Tiffani. Every day at lunch, Tiffani had to give the lunch lady a yellow ticket. We all knew what that meant. Tiffani's family was "poor." I had no intention of finding out what I needed to do to actually receive the reduced-price lunch benefit. I wanted nothing to do with any markers that would signal my new, lower status. I bought my lunch with the cash that was left from my paychecks.

In the cafeteria, there was the standard hot lunch line on one side, but there was also an à la carte stand in a separate open space in the middle of the cafeteria. The à la carte stand sold mini-pizzas, french fries, nachos, candy bars, and other junk food, but they only accepted cash. Because the food prices were higher at the à la carte stand, it was an unspoken truth that the hot lunch line was for the low-income kids. As a result, for months I made a beeline for the à la carte stand to conspicuously pay for my lunch. One day, though, I wanted a baked potato, and those were only available by going through the hot lunch line. I carefully counted out the change I needed ($1.25) and got into line to pay for my potato. When I got to the front of the line, the woman working the register told me what I owed. *Thirty-five cents.* She never skipped a beat, nor did her expression give away a flicker of recognition. My body went cold. My face flushed. I heard a rushing sound in my ears. I thought I might faint. Surely, I must have heard her wrong. I asked her to repeat herself. She did. The amount had not changed, and neither did her expression. I hurriedly handed her the money and rushed out of the line. I could only hope that no one else had heard.

I returned to the table where my friends were, but I couldn't eat. How could this woman who had never met me and who didn't know anything about me know my most intimate secret—the one secret that I had worked so hard to hide from everyone? In a school of twenty-six hundred students, how could she possibly have associated my name on a piece of paper for the reduced-price lunch program with the girl standing in front of her? And more important, if my charade hadn't fooled her, had it fooled anyone else? I was panicked, ashamed, and scared. During this time, I saw many of the changes that occurred as structural things that were happening to me, but I did not think that these events reflected anything about me personally. For the first time since our economic downward slide began, someone had looked at me and seen the truth.

I was convinced it was a mistake, but it took me months to work up the courage to go back and try again. I dressed carefully that day, making sure I was obviously wearing my most expensive outfit and that my hair and makeup were flawless. I attempted to be breezy and unconcerned, but I was panicked inside. As I inched closer to the register with my potato, my heart beat wildly. By the time I got to the front of the line, I was convinced I would hear the "right" amount from her. She couldn't possibly look at me and think that I was "poor." I was sure it wasn't going to happen again. But it did. *Thirty-five cents.* I never went back through the hot food line again.

Two years later I graduated and left for college. I attended a small, wealthy liberal arts college on scholarship, where I continued to hide my social class just as carefully as I did in high school. I told only a few trusted friends about my family's situation, and it wasn't until my senior year that I felt comfortable enough to invite my college roommate to visit my family. I continued to work small jobs to buy my clothing and to pay for the things I wanted. I did everything I could to pretend that I was just like everyone else. I avoided doing anything that would betray my social class.

I think one of the privileges of being middle class is that I don't remember thinking about money until we didn't have it. Yet it wasn't until I entered graduate school and I took a class on "Stigma and Prejudice" that I started to critically examine my experiences crossing back and forth between social classes. I began to think a lot about my experience in the cafeteria and what it taught me about the stigma of poverty: how poverty can be visible, invisible, or become visible over the course of an interaction. I've thought about how certain signs are used as markers of social class, and how one's identity can be tied to those signs. I've pondered the psychological and social consequences of poverty for children, as well as the messages that are taught to them about the relationship between education, hard work, and the American dream.

And I've thought about the lunch lady herself. I never learned how she did it. I suspect that she looked up the yearbook pictures of all the kids who qualified for the free/reduced-price lunch program and memorized their faces, but I'll never be sure. At the time, I wanted nothing to do with her. Now I wish I could talk to her—to ask her how she did it, to ask her why she did it, but most of all to thank her for her kindness.

PART II

Working Class

IN THE UNITED STATES, THE CONCEPT OF
"working class" is politically charged. Politicians and
mainstream media commentators are loath to use the
term, and when they even mention class, it is invariably
preceded by "middle." In contrast to European and Latin
American societies, which tend to be more class conscious
and less inhibited by class-explicit language, the norm in the
United States assumes a society unencumbered by class
divisions. If class is to be discussed, Americans are portrayed
as overwhelmingly middle class, and political figures,
whether Democratic or Republican, invariably pitch their
policies as ones that will foster a strong middle class.

Interestingly, in surveys measuring Americans' class
identification, when given a choice between choosing middle
or working class, Americans split, and 44 percent call
themselves middle class, while the same percentage choose
working class.[1] This suggests that while the taboo against

---

1. Shawn Fremstead, "America's Invisible–and Very Diverse–Working Class," Center for Economic and Policy Research, February 21, 2014, http://www.cepr.net/index.php/blogs/cepr-blog/americas-invisibleand-very-diverseworking-class.

admitting there are classes in the United States may dominate among political and media elites, rank-and-file Americans admit to a different world.

While social scientists who study class generally include the working class as one of a number of classes in the United States, they differ as to its size. For economists and sociologists with a Marxist perspective, the United States has a "working class majority,"[2] as the vast bulk of the population works for someone else, has little or no authority on the job, and possesses little real wealth. Most social scientists do not measure class based on one's relationship to the means of production, but rather see class along a continuum, with some, for example, possessing more wealth, more education, more authority, and more prestige. And so one can move up and down the class hierarchy, as more or fewer of the key resources are won or lost. For these researchers, one can climb from working poor to working class to lower middle class, and so on. While this type of approach validates the reality of a working class, the middle class ends up being the most populous group.[3]

In this part of the book, some of the contributors explicitly state their working-class identification, while others discuss aspects of their class upbringing or viewpoints that would seem to place them in the working class. About half of our working-class sample have experienced mobility from a more hardscrabble economic lifestyle. They point to higher education as the means that afforded them a more secure economic status. For this reason, we have grouped several of the stories linked to higher education into a subsection, "Working Class and College." The rest don't discuss education per se, but in the stories they reflect on one or more attributes of working-class identification.

Beginning first with the "reflective" submissions, Tim Harris's description of warehouse work makes clear the distinction between

---

2. Michael Zweig, *The Working Class Majority: America's Best Kept Secret*, 2nd ed. (Ithaca: Cornell University Press, 2012); James W. Russell, *Class and Race Formation in North America* (Toronto: University of Toronto Press, 2009).

3. Diana Kendall, *Framing Class: Media Representations of Wealth and Poverty in America*, 2nd ed. (Lanham, MD: Rowman & Littlefield, 2011).

the life of hourly workers and management, not just in attitudes, pay, and working conditions, but also in access to something as basic as decent toilet facilities. Memories of the value of hard work are shared in several working-class reminiscences, and one writer, Dwight Lang, proudly remembers his father, a lifelong construction worker, and his working-class town, as he angrily disputes a right-wing talk show host's mocking condescension toward "those of us from Rio Linda." In a memoir about her elderly grandmother, Karen Estrella reminds us of the value of craftsmanship, whether it be in maintaining well-scrubbed floors or in cooking. Food plays a significant role in one's class or status, and N. Jeanne Burns, in reflecting on her own working-class background, explains how an artichoke means more than "just sustenance." Several authors, including Karen Spector and Michaelann Bewsee, help us to understand class distinctions—specifically the difference between poor and working class—by focusing on the importance of having a car, an apartment of one's own, or access to health care.

While many from the working-class sample made it through college and graduate school to enter the ranks of higher education faculty, themes of discomfort emerge from their stories. Having worked hard and proved they had the right stuff, and now situated in what should be a gentle world where ideas and fair play dominate, they wonder if they really belong. In his book *Limbo: Blue-Collar Roots, White-Collar Dreams*, Alfred Lubrano calls this group "straddlers," as they straddle the worlds between their working-class origins and new middle-class status and prestige.[4]

Straddlers often feel like they no longer have a home. Camisha Jones writes, "I am now someone whose consciousness spans two distinct worlds: a world of financial sufficiency and one of plenty." As Christine Overall sums it up, "Almost every time I give a public lecture, lead a workshop, or I teach a class, I'm afraid of failure . . . the revelation that I do not belong in the class I worked so hard to enter." Like Overall, K. Stricker works her way up to a faculty position, only

---

4. Alfred Lubrano, *Limbo: Blue-Collar Roots, White-Collar Dreams* (Hoboken, NJ: John Wiley & Sons, 2004).

to discover that her background and current position aren't viewed favorably by her colleagues. "The realization that I don't have the right pedigree has been painful, as has the understanding that in the eyes of many of the members of the academy, I am still a member of the 'lower' class."

As some advanced on the road to graduate degrees and faculty positions, their new status brought them misunderstanding and even resentment from their families of origin, a not uncommon reaction facing straddlers. Jennifer O'Connor Duffy's extended family "ridiculed" her applications to elite liberal arts colleges, and when she was accepted at Amherst College, they "resented" her. The grandparents who raised John Rosario-Perez "squashed my ambitions as being unrealistic and far-fetched. . . . Knowingly, they warned me that I would never fit in." Yet there are also stories of well-meaning relatives who try to help their upwardly mobile family members, and who learn to appreciate their gestures, even if it takes a number of years.

In her freshman year of college, Janet Casey received a gift box from her grandfather ("a sixty-eight-year-old truck driver with an eighth-grade education"), filled with supplies for her room, supplies that he decided she would need after comparing her side of the room with her roommate's during a campus visit. At the time, she didn't like the gifts, including a desk lamp, as "his efforts seemed ill-conceived and embarrassing—reminders of a past from which I was already trying to distance myself." Looking back now, she realizes that her grandfather was only trying "to alleviate" the "material differences" that he saw in her side of the room. Now, the gift seems like "a precious thing, a lifeline thrown haphazardly to a child who seemed in some way needy, from a grandfather who could not quite interpret the need but who wanted to provide in whatever way he could."

Schooling often served as a harsh version of basic training for these straddlers in learning about class, class conflict, and differing class values. Class shame and embarrassment could lead to hiding one's class origin on a middle-class campus. "Looking back," remembers John Rosario-Perez, "I realize that through sheer force of will I 'out-middle-classed' my middle-class schoolmates. Ultimately, my impersonation was to make me a stranger to them, for it prohibited me from revealing anything personal from beyond the confines of our shared world."

But, for some, the struggle continues, and the journey for authenticity is realized. Michelle Tokarczyk had incorporated some of the negativity shown to working-class students as they pursued undergraduate and graduate degrees. "The times when I felt working class were the times when I felt alienated, ostracized from and distinctly different from my middle-class peers. Being middle class . . . meant belonging . . . enjoying the rewards of life . . . and the approval of those around you." After a good deal of introspection, she decided to come out as a working-class academic, and in 1988 developed a panel on working-class women in the academy at a major conference. "To my greater surprise, the small room was packed, standing room only. People crowded the halls outside." These women were "testifying" to the validity of their working-class roots, intent to stay in higher education and to make their "experience visible." We learn that some of the other authors, men as well as women, who had uneasy paths to higher education positions have also come out as working-class academics, thus ensuring that current and future generations of working-class students will have class role models.

Those of Us from Rio Linda

DWIGHT LANG

The windowless room at Sunset Lawn Funeral Home is cold and overwhelmingly quiet. I stand back looking at his face and almost don't recognize him. For a brief, terrifying moment I imagine his eyes opening to stare at me. The shapes of nearby objects shift as I sit down to get a closer look. He seems small, his thin body hidden under a white sheet. Pungent chemical odors betray futile attempts to preserve human appearance.

He would be dressed in his only suit. It is blue. There'd be no tie, of course. Dad was uncomfortable wearing ties. Plumbers wear suits and ties on special occasions. Men who regularly dress this way live and die in other parts of town.

I imagine his lungs filled with asbestos after a lifetime working construction. Those who completed the autopsy saw his lungs, but I'm not going to look under the sheet at his sewed-up chest. Oddly, I remember his Fort Ord, misty Monterey Bay, army boot-camp stories about training to invade Japan.

Suddenly I need to get out of there. Outside I breathe more easily and feel the July Sacramento heat I grew up with and escaped. I clamber into the car rental—a midsize maroon Ford—picked up after flying from Michigan. Where do I go from here? Two miles up the road is a small town where I had been raised.

Rio Linda hasn't changed much over the years. Economic development passed over the community where I played Little

League. There's the baseball diamond where I shagged grounders—dreaming of glory. Still, I'm curious heading up Dry Creek Road. Our double-wide trailer on Kenora Street is severely faded. I buy a cold Coke at Nu Way Market on Front Street, where Mom waitressed in the early 1960s.

I notice the old house that had been the county library. It was never fancy, but I treasured those musty smells, sunlight streaming between rows of old books, and the suspicious eyes of the part-time librarian. Dorothy stamped due dates in my books about distant, imaginary worlds.

I left Rio Linda and moved to places with names like Berkeley, Eugene, and Ann Arbor. Others, many just like me, were forced to, didn't, or couldn't leave. We all had dreams—pursued and realized, set aside and lost.

Rush Limbaugh abruptly interrupts my drift to memory. The radio station playing music is featuring Limbaugh's commentary on a jailed journalist who refuses to name names.

I knew about Rush's early reputation at KFBK radio in the late 1980s—giving views on news and people he didn't know. He routinely mocked Rio Linda for its white-trash, trailer-park ways: cars up on blocks, welfare and unemployment all around. In typical condescending manner Rush simplifies 2005 events surrounding covert CIA agent Valerie Plame with the patronizing phrase he coined and still enjoys using: "For those of you in Rio Linda . . ." These hicks and hillbillies need things explained to them.

Rush demeans less-affluent Americans he and others hope will join America's volunteer military. How many other working-class communities send their young off to war under Rush's approving gaze?

I think about veterans constructing homes for people like Rush. But we never hear his tales of Rio Lindans laboring in the heat and cold, breathing asbestos. "For those of you in Rio Linda . . ."

I wonder about the irony, as Rush jabbers on about brave people fighting for freedom. I recall the army ethic sarcastically repeated by Dad over the years: "Ours not to reason why, ours but to do or die."

Yet those I grew up around understood politics and economics. Some even read literature. I remember declarations of pride in contributions to America, but also recall their resentment with how some outsiders view Rio Linda: a place filled with Git-R-Done, trailer-trash, no-nothings. I wonder how this might play out in upcoming elections, especially as blue-collar jobs continue vanishing overseas.

Would Rio Lindans around the country end up bitter, disillusioned with neocon policies and conservative pundits? But Rush never bothers to stop by and ask our opinion. He probably assumes we'd never reason why. "For those of you in Rio Linda . . ."

Dad seldom trusted anyone with a college degree. He took great pleasure in using colorful words to describe political and cultural elites who manipulate the nation. Those words lurk beneath the surface of my middle-class ways. Finishing my drive through Rio Linda I thought about Dad stirring back at Sunset Lawn. I imagined his face and usual sneer.

The Cost of Passing

JOHN ROSARIO-PEREZ

By the time I was nine years old I had become acutely aware of the link between intelligence and social class. I soon came to understand that knowledge was a commodity and that intelligence conferred special status.

Despite the egalitarian disguise of our Catholic school uniforms, you could easily discern the "haves" from the "have nots" if you looked below the surface. The distinction was made not only on the basis of appearance but of attitude. For example, the better-off students boasted of being financially rewarded for their good grades—a dollar for every A—when report cards were handed out. Meanwhile, the rest of us rarely received any praise from our families for our grades. At school these "bright" children enjoyed a special status, elevated in both stature and grace far above their classmates. Blessed by fate, the well-to-do, it turned out, were not only smarter than the rest of us, they were also holier.

Early on, I aimed to emulate these intelligent and "gifted" children. Unaware of my own motives, I set out on an extended plan of self-improvement, striving to make good grades without recognizing that envy, shame, and ambition—and not a love of learning—underlay my efforts.

Raised by Midwestern, working-class grandparents, I often felt strangely out of sorts at home and at school. My grandfather, a land surveyor, was the ostensible breadwinner in our family, although it often seemed that he stayed home more days than he worked. A bitter and defeated man, he provided with me a certain slant on working-class identity, one based on reactionary attitudes, male dominance, and a kind of fatuous heroism—qualities common to the stereotypical blue-collar hero. He was a more intemperate version of Archie Bunker, a bigot without a sense of humor. He, too, despised unions, thought FDR had ruined the country, and believed that granting civil rights to blacks would destroy the nation. A dyed-in-the-wool Republican, he voted outside of his party affiliation only once—when George Wallace ran for president on a platform of reversing civil rights. Simply put, class consciousness did not exist in his worldview. By dint of his military service during World War II, he believed that he was not poor but very much a part of the mainstream.

Indeed, my grandfather truly was an "army of one" and ruled the house with an autocratic sternness: he viewed women and children with equal contempt; forbade small talk at the dinner table; enforced frugality as the highest virtue; and was not above using physical punishment for infractions major and minor. More often than not he dominated the living room sitting in his underwear and belching loudly while he drank beer. Our home resembled the crude world of military barracks, except that only one of us was a solider. A full set of his false teeth adorned various ledges, mantels, and cupboards throughout the house, offering evidence of his daily ritual of sliding his dentures in, grimacing with pain, and then quickly sliding them out with a terse "Goddamn it." Hypochondriacal and impassive, he spent much of his free time at doctors' offices in search of a cure for his elusive ailments.

He remained emotionally distant and therefore perpetually mysterious and intimidating to me. He said few words, but when he spoke my grandmother and I listened and obeyed without question. He had no friends and few casual social contacts. His one real pleasure was reading, and each week he ventured to the library, borrowed a raft of books, and spent the week buried in yet another volume of World War II history, alternating between the European and Asian theaters of war. He had read hundreds of such books by the time I had graduated from high school, but he never once recounted his own war experiences to me. We did not have one full conversation during my entire childhood. Instead, he relived the war in the private domain of memory and literature, or reminisced with my grandmother about the life they had left behind in the Midwest.

My grandfather resented many people, particularly those who had less materially or were different because of their race or nationality. A long list of miscreants, it included me for being half Puerto Rican and in need of his pity throughout most of my childhood. In his mind my mother had ruined her life by marrying my father, and I was the unfortunate outcome; blameless perhaps, but unfortunate nevertheless. By the time I could say my first words, my father was long gone, pushed out of the fold by my racist grandparents.

In those days, my grandmother—still alive at ninety-seven—was a short, stout woman with silver hair whose shoes often bore the remnant of a china marker on their soles: twenty-five cents. She scoured secondhand clothing stores with a pauper's acuity. She was both charismatic and chimerical. Her large personality and iron will belied her physical stature. With little effort, she could be refined and gracious in public, her voice warm, sympathetic, and motherly. At home she could be altogether different, alternating between impatient fury and humor. To mete out punishment she often chased me with a vinyl flyswatter, cornering me and then repeatedly aiming at my bare legs until I trembled in tears. My crime, in her eyes, was my disrespect in not obeying her rules, arbitrary and petty as they often seemed. In this she was like the nuns at school, who also relied on corporal punishment.

To relax, my grandmother often sat on the porch smoking a corncob pipe or held court at the kitchen table, reading people's fortunes with a deck of playing cards. She surrounded herself with a retinue of female friends, many of whom she had befriended when she worked for a catering company. Some were widowed, others divorced (relatively uncommon in those days). Some lived with boyfriends (even more uncommon), and each had a story. I remember Mrs. W, whose dentures slid in her mouth when she spoke, giving her a pronounced sibilant lisp. She had a piercing laugh, high-pitched and raucous, and I remember thinking, even as a young boy, that Mrs. W must be hiding something of which she cannot speak, her laughter providing a cover for what, I did not know. There was Bertha, who tended bar at one of the beer joints downtown. She stood out because of a scar that went from ear to ear, the result of being knifed during a brawl. Next door to us lived Old Lady Tate, who responded to schoolboys' antics by standing on her porch with her revolver drawn.

But most memorable was my grandmother's friend Verna Brown, a self-proclaimed hillbilly from the coal mining country of West Virginia. From the very start, Verna fascinated me. I loved the smell of pinto beans cooking on her stove, the homemade tortillas she toasted on an open flame, and the bright-orange log of welfare cheese that she got from God knows where. I especially cherished the handmade quilt she sewed personally for me. Some thought her the epitome of white trash, her house stacked from floor to ceiling with boxes and junk. She, too, wore secondhand clothes, and was missing a couple of front teeth on her bridge. Truth be told, Verna was as shrewd a businesswoman as she was unpretentious. She owned a number of houses and collected a reasonable income from the rent, although she continued to work as a short-order cook.

Besides her profound practicality, Verna was also blessed with a sixth sense. Like my grandmother, she told fortunes, but with more acuity and nuance. Perhaps she had been my grandmother's mentor. Whereas my grandmother spoke of fortune-telling as a hobby, Verna was a bona fide psychic—hook, line, and sinker. She held séances on the weekends, and her daughter, while in a trance, drew pastel portraits of spirit guides, the most prominent being Blue Belle, a young slave girl who watched over Verna and communicated from the other side. She had no doubt that these messages were divinely inspired.

My grandfather, a confirmed atheist, disdained talk of psychic phenomena as evidence of my grandmother's intellectual inferiority. To defend the veracity of Verna's premonitions, my grandmother often told the story of the day Verna dropped by and exclaimed, "Mona, why haven't you packed your suitcase? You're going on a trip. Your daughter needs you." In my grandmother's version, the phone rang later that afternoon. An aunt who lived in Texas called to report that her entire family had come down with a severe case of hepatitis and needed my grandmother to come and nurse them back to health.

As much as she believed in the spirit world, my grandmother harbored a zealous mistrust of doctors or "quacks," as she called them. Instead, she conjured home remedies, often under Verna's tutelage. For a cough, she made onion syrup; a mustard plaster for bronchitis; a mild wash of boric acid healed cuts and wounds. But doctors were men with dollar signs in their eyes, and she resented my grandfather for spending his spare income on doctors rather than on us.

In my earlier years, I accepted at face value the characters who peopled my childhood. They were the people I knew best. But on reaching adolescence I became painfully aware that I was from "the wrong side of the tracks," and my attempts to succeed in school paled with my determination to conceal my home life from my classmates. Concurrently, my grandparents squashed my ambitions for being unrealistic and far-fetched, and in defiance I was determined to "show them." Knowingly, they warned me that I would never fit in. As a result of their fatalistic attitude, I became more private and secretive about my intellectual pursuits.

Perpetually conflicted about my social class, I created as wide a berth as possible between my various worlds to hide real and imagined disparities. Even if I could "pass" in the classroom, I felt that my personal life betrayed me and exposed the ruse. The evidence of my poverty, from my secondhand clothing to our tattered and patched furniture, felt malignant. Back at school, I befriended students who represented everything I wanted out of life: summer vacations, their own homes, assurance of attending college if for no other reason than that their parents had—a list that now seems like a modest set of privileges. Looking back, I realize that through sheer force of will I "out-middle-classed" my middle-class schoolmates. Ultimately, my impersonation was to make me a stranger to them, for it prohibited me from revealing anything personal from beyond the confines of our shared world.

The Floors of the Met

KAREN ESTRELLA

About ten years ago I took my grandmother, my *abuela*, to the Metropolitan Museum of Art in New York City. To most New Yorkers, this amazing institution is affectionately known as "the Met." My grandmother had never been to the Met. She was one of those Old World people who never go out for "entertainment." These are people who still unplug all appliances and electronics when they are not being used. These people never buy something they don't really need, barely speak English, and always think you have never eaten enough. My grandmother has never been to the movies, or to a concert, and certainly had not been to a museum.

I don't want you to get the wrong impression about her. She was someone who appreciated the aesthetics of a thing well made. For all of her working years, she was a seamstress. She could make anything. As a child I watched her cut patterns out of newspaper, and then with discipline and determination make a suit you'd be proud to wear. Up until her stroke at the age of eighty-nine, she never wore a store-bought dress. I believe even her undergarments were made by her own hand. And no fabric was unsalvageable. When I was eight she made me, and my doll, the loveliest dress I ever owned from the drapes that used to hang in her living room. My doll still wore that dress long after I had moved away to college.

She was a simple woman. She lived on the ninth floor of her apartment building in the South Bronx from 1960 to 2007, and for more than forty years (until her stroke) she only occasionally took the elevator, preferring to walk the stairs. She believed in shopping every day for the food you'd need that day, and when she cooked a chicken, she caressed it clean, as if it were a baby, preparing it for a bath of garlic, onions, salt, pepper, oregano, cilantro, and oil.

Over the course of her ninety-two years, she had only been in a car a dozen times. She came to New York City on a boat when she was eighteen, and only began to travel outside the city in the 1980s after her last living sister moved from Brooklyn to the Catskills. I think they moved, my great aunt and her husband, to have more room for the chickens. My great aunt Mercedes always raised chickens—she for the meat, and her husband for the cockfighting. The only other time I remember my grandmother traveling out of the city was to attend the funeral of her eldest son, my father, when he died at the age of forty-six, in New Jersey.

Before my dad moved to New Jersey, he lived in Brooklyn. I moved there too, when I was twenty-two, to spend a year doing an unpaid music therapy internship at Flower Hospital, a hospital for developmentally disabled children and adults on the Upper East Side of Manhattan, just blocks from Museum Mile. From 82nd Street to 105th Street along Fifth Avenue, New York City has designated the area "Museum Mile" because of the many museums and fine art institutions that line Central Park. In those days, the museums along the mile opened up on Thursday evenings for free. And I would go.

There is no better refuge, after a hard day's work, than a walk into the circular structure of the Guggenheim, or a time travel through the past in the Museum of the City of New York, or a rest on a bench in one of the many courtyards within the Met. The only evening better than Thursdays on Museum Mile involved a trip to my grandmother's for a home-cooked dinner. I would try to go once a week. It was only three stops on the train.

The Upper East Side and the South Bronx are quite close, and I would often take the train there to visit with my grandmother after work. I would tell her about my day, about the museums, about the movies I'd seen, or the books I was reading. While it was always a short ride to the Bronx, getting back to Brooklyn took a couple of hours by train. Despite the long trip, I came to think of it as short once I moved to Boston.

After moving to Boston, I began to come down and stay with my grandmother on the weekends about six or seven times a year. I would arrive on Friday night or Saturday morning. I'd rise early Saturday to do something in the city: visit a friend, go to the Village, walk the streets of Chinatown. My grandmother always stayed home to cook. She never understood the appeal of restaurants.

After I was married I brought my husband along too. On Saturdays, we usually took the train into Manhattan, which was much easier than driving and parking. Sometimes I just hung out with my grandmother in the afternoon, but inevitably I'd tell her not to cook for us. My husband and I looked forward to trying new restaurants in the city. Dinner and a movie proved a great Saturday night pastime. We'd promise not to be home too late, as her neighborhood wasn't safe at night.

In the morning, we'd awaken to a breakfast of eggs, Puerto Rican corn fritters called *arepas*, bacon, café Bustelo, and orange juice, before making our way to the museum. Sunday in New York was museum day for me once I had moved to Boston. After having kids I'd kept the routine simple. Come down Saturday night, stay over, wake up Sunday morning, eat our Puerto Rican breakfast, and go to the museum. Each time I would ask my abuela if she wanted to go with us. She always said no. Why would she go to Manhattan? For twenty years she had been saying no, and given that she was now in her eighties, this would mean taking the car, and she hated cars. She'd have to dress up, and people would see her. She would be out in the world; they'd laugh at her teeth.

But one Sunday she decided to go. I think her curiosity finally caught up with her. She just had to know what this "museum" visit we made every time we were in New York was all about. I think the fact that the kids went gave her courage. If young children could go, so could she. So, she put on her best coat—a coat she had made of checkered black-and-white wool, with special buttons—over her best dress, one made from store-bought cloth, not the drapes she had used in the past, and her best black stockings with a black scarf over her head. In her day, ladies did not go out without their heads covered.

We drove the 3.8 miles from my abuela's house to the Met, found a parking space right on Fifth Avenue, and walked down toward the museum. Now you have to understand my excitement and near panic when my grandmother said yes. I felt an enormous sense of responsibility to make this visit right. I knew that once she had come with me to the museum, she would never come again. That this was the one time in a lifetime of living in New York that she would indulge me in my need to bring her along.

I felt so nervous. I thought—well, we'll go to a few rooms. I knew I couldn't overdo it, especially since my kids at the time were still quite young, three and five years old. We'd stay about an hour and go to the cafeteria, where we'd get coffee and a snack. This last part of the plan was risky. I knew my grandmother would be scornful about the coffee. According to her, Americans drink brown water, not coffee, and as far as she's concerned, you can never trust a restaurant kitchen. They don't know anything about food—how to prepare it with love and care, not to mention enough flavor. They don't bathe their chickens, and restaurant kitchens in her mind were filthy!

As we drove down to Manhattan, I became racked with worry about which room to take her to. The Met can be an overwhelming place, even for me, and I had been going there for over twenty years. The place could seem like so much to take in, so much to marvel at, so much to absorb. The responsibility of deciding which art would be the only art she would ever see was nearly overwhelming.

I was sweating. Should I take her to something modern? Picasso is amazing! I kept thinking that perhaps something from his blue period would speak to her. The Guggenheim has a picture of the woman ironing from Picasso's blue period in its permanent collection, and it had always reminded me of her life. But we were not going to the Guggenheim.

Perhaps it would be best if I took her to the American wing, with its Tiffany windows and open courtyard, its wonderful sculptures and breathtaking paintings by Homer, Sargent, and the American landscape artists. To get there we'd go through the Hall of Armor, and she might enjoy those soldiers and horses.

Or perhaps I should take her to the Greek or Roman sections—just think of all those large sculptures that had endured all these years. Classical beauty. Or maybe even something exotic—like her; how about the Japanese art?

No, I decided that I would take her to the impressionists. Pears, haystacks, sunflowers, and cathedrals—these were scenes she could understand and appreciate. And I so wanted to share with her those gentle, soft lines.

As we passed the fountain in front of the museum and climbed up the front steps leading into the amazing rotunda, I found myself holding my breath. We walked into that grand atrium and I said, "Abuela, look at these flower arrangements. There are ladies who do these every few weeks, new flowers, imagine. Aren't they something?" She stood close by, hunched a bit over, hoping no one was noticing her teeth or her person, and we mounted the stairs to the impressionist rooms.

"What do you think, Abuela?" I asked.

"The floors are beautiful" she answered.

The floors? But the walls, Abuela? The paintings on the walls? "Oh yes . . . they are nice."

Was it that she knew that someone had to clean these floors? Was it the wood and polish that she noticed? Was it easier to look down than up?

"Oh, and now I see how so many restaurants can stay open," she added. In her generation, you knew it took hours to cook a good meal. Women should stay home to cook for their families, not do frivolous things like walk around a museum, and yet there were hundreds of people here. Now she understood why so many restaurants survived in the city.

I can't tell you the month or time of year that I took my grandmother to the museum. I can't tell you what snack we had with our "bad" coffee that day. And at the end of her life my *abuelita* sat in a wheelchair from the stroke that she suffered a few years before, making it hard to remember the way she had bounded up those nine flights of stairs. But when I remember that day, I see her holding my arm and walking with me through that atrium up the stairs of the Met. I feel the weight of her arm on my forearm. I can remember that, and the day that the floors of the museum meant more to me than any painting that hung on the walls.

Washroom Class Politics

TIMOTHY HARRIS

I discovered my class anger in 1983. I was twenty-two and working at an auto parts warehouse in Cambridge, Massachusetts. I'd just been discharged from a four-year air force hitch and, in the fall, would leave for Amherst to attend the University of Massachusetts. I lied to get the job. College was my secret, for me to know and for them to find out.

Enlistment in the air force had been my ticket out of Sioux Falls, South Dakota. The city's two meatpacking plants offered the rare union wage in a right-to-work state, and the rich smell that hung in the air, we all thought, was a small price to pay for a shot at the middle class. While these jobs were hard to get, finding work—with no benefits and at around minimum wage—was relatively easy, even for a high school dropout like me.

By the age of nineteen I'd washed dishes, dug ditches in hard red clay, done landscaping and farm labor, piled potatoes into fifteen-foot mountains, and assembled mobile home rafters at the rate of forty-five an hour. It was this last job, held for nearly a year, that drove me into the military.

I was the youngest person in the factory, and my future could be easily discerned in those around me. Repetitive, mind-numbing labor, made bearable by arriving stoned and using our three breaks a day to stay high. The family men sold dope on the side to make ends meet, and the rest of us saved up for a set of chrome mags, or maybe a Marantz stereo.

After a year of this, the military was looking pretty good. I took my GED and enlisted, enticed by visions of air-conditioned office work and a steady paycheck. From my station at Hanscom AFB in Bedford, Massachusetts, I enrolled in community college and eventually applied to UMass. Miraculously, I was accepted. I just had to survive one more summer of crappy work.

I found a room in Waltham with a shared bathroom in the hall and took a job at Action Crash Parts in Cambridge as their warehouse guy. I worked alone, pulling radiators and such off the ten-foot-high shelves and binding orders together on pallets for delivery. My boss was a recent college grad who'd majored in business and spoke just enough Mandarin to negotiate wholesale prices from China. While he worked the phones in his air-conditioned office, temperatures in the warehouse would turn the dust that settled on my skin to slow-running mud.

A deeper circle of hell than my own existed in the bumper re-chroming operation a floor below. Here, non-English-speaking immigrants from Haiti, Mexico, and El Salvador toiled in unbearable temperatures amid toxic chemicals for roughly the same non-livable wage. We shared a filthy washroom, which management refused to clean. The front office bathroom, reserved for the bosses and the young white women who worked just outside the office's plate-glass windows, had perfumed soap, Charmin, and nice lighting.

This, I decided, was the bathroom for me. Occasionally, someone would point out that I belonged upstairs, in the stench-filled workers' toilet, where we were to wipe our asses with rough paper towels. I'd stare blankly and nod. They thought I was too stupid to comprehend. I was going to college. Fuck 'em. I'd shit where I wanted. Eventually, they gave up.

My badly rusted Saab had been good for a one-way trip to Cambridge before the temperature needle edged into the red. My minimum-wage earnings paid for rent, gas, cigarettes, and just enough food to get by. There was no money for car repairs. About a month into the job, I complained about my wages to my Mandarin-speaking boss.

He was clearly annoyed. "What do you need to live?" he asked. The question took me by surprise. I forget my answer, but whatever I said, it rated another forty cents an hour. A few years later, as a social theory and political economy major at UMass, I would learn that wages within capitalism are calculated to provide for the bare reproduction of labor power. This struck me as more or less self-evident.

One day during lunch break, a few blocks from where I worked, I stumbled across the Revolutionary Communist Party bookstore. The guy behind the counter struck up a conversation. As I stood there, skinny and hungry and with dirt lodged deep in my pores, I no doubt excited feelings of solidarity. I felt something as well. Here was a place that spoke to what I was beginning to feel, but still was completely foreign soil. I had no words but wanted to understand.

"Take this and read it," he said, "and then come back and we'll talk." He handed me a thin tan paperback. It was V. I. Lenin's *On Imperialism*. Later, alone in my one room, the connection between Lenin's treatise on the economics of war and my own poverty escaped me. I never went back. The man in the bookstore clearly didn't get it.

I came clean with Mandarin-guy a week before my departure to Amherst. He took the news philosophically. As a farewell gesture, he bought me lunch. This just pissed me off even more. Suddenly, I was no longer the warehouse rat. I was college bound, with my new status as a near-peer being sealed over pizza.

The difference between us, I thought, cannot be erased this easily. There was another thought as well. College will not turn me into him. I might change, but the past would come along with me.

Artichokes

N. JEANNE BURNS

A friend said recently that one definitive marker of social class is whether you know how to eat an artichoke. This probably isn't true for migrant farmworkers who toil in or around Castroville, California, the self-proclaimed "Artichoke Capital of the World." Or even for people who grew up on the Mediterranean, where the plant is native. But M. F. K. Fisher, who herself grew up surrounded by fields of artichokes, recognized the class-climbing rank of the thistle in her essay "The Social Status of the Vegetable." And the distinction feels right to me, even seventy years later, despite other, more elite foods like pâté de fois gras making a clear status statement. Maybe it's because you can get artichoke hearts on home-delivered pizza or in jars at even some of the smallest grocery stores. But the flower itself is hard to find and looks threatening when you spy it on your produce shelves.

I don't recall the first time I tasted an artichoke, sometime in my twenties. It was probably in a dip, the vegetable's real flavor and texture drowned out by mayonnaise, cheese, and canned artichoke brine. However, I remember the first time I saw an artichoke in the grocery store, looking more like a wall of soldiers guarding the asparagus than the tender delicious vegetable I would come to love. I pretended to examine grapefruit while I watched several people pick through the bin and place two or four blooms in their carts.

I was embarrassed because people around me seemed to know something I didn't: how to turn that oversized green pinecone into a meal.

I couldn't ask my mother, because she wouldn't know. She'd grown up in Appalachian rural poverty and ate only what her family could grow. Artichokes didn't appear on their table.

Knowing scarcity herself, she made sure our working-class family always had sustenance but never cooked more than we could eat at one sitting. The food stayed within the boundaries of her experience. Fried chicken. Canned green beans and raw bacon boiled together for half an hour. Fried pork chops. Collards and bacon fat, cooked until the greens were wilted, dark and shiny with grease. Fried salmon cakes made with fish from a tin. Canned peas boiled to mush. Mom kept a large tin of bacon grease by the stove to fry eggs, make gravy, and glaze biscuits. Her spice cabinet held only salt, pepper, and cream of tartar. She hated garlic.

I've come to love more subtle tastes and textures than my mother taught me to appreciate.

In my early thirties, I went with friends to a restaurant I'd heard was very good. The waiter brought tiny plates to our celebratory table. On each, a minute crouton cradling a smear of fresh mozzarella was covered with a fresh basil leaf and drizzled with a sweet brown liquid.

"An *amuse-bouche* from the chef," he said, "topped with balsamic vinegar."

We'd been waiting over an hour for the last of the party to arrive and were very hungry. By the time my friends and I downed the diminutive appetizers, wiped our mouths and returned the napkins to our respective laps, we wanted more and let the waiter know.

He laughed. "That was one-hundred-year-old balsamic—$250 per ounce."

Its velvety sweet flavor hinted at a heavy red wine, but with a subtly sharp vinegar taste in the background. I'd never tasted something so good or so expensive. I wanted more.

After that dinner, for very special times my partner Liz and I wanted to mark, we splurged at restaurants where haricots verts are slender green beans, charcuterie is a selection of shaved deli meats, coulis is a thin sauce. I never liked steak until I felt my first bite of filet mignon melting on my tongue. And you would never have seen me eat a parsnip until I had tasted pureed root vegetables at a local French restaurant.

I don't tell Mom about my food escapades because I'm certain she'd be offended at the amount of money we spend on a dinner for two and be worried about how I dressed. "You wore hose and a slip, I hope," she'd say, the *o* in hope drawn out as if there were a *u* after it. She never wanted her social class to show and taught me to mimic people I judged to be a higher class than I, as she had.

When my mother told me she first used a napkin when she was fifteen, in 1960, I had a lot of questions. What did she use to wipe her mouth before 1960? (An arm or sleeve.) Did all her friends and schoolmates wipe their mouths with their sleeves? (Yes.) And, finally, how did she learn to use a napkin?

An upper-middle-class family had come into the hills seeking a live-in babysitter and found my mother. She moved away from her family for the first time to take this summer job. When Mom was asked to set the table, she was told to set out napkins (she doesn't remember whether they were cloth or paper). She watched the family members wipe their mouths. She mimicked their actions, inferring correctly that people in a class above hers use napkins.

My neighborhood housed firefighters, truck drivers, and janitors, so I first encountered middle-class people in college. Since then, I've observed and mimicked cultural mores many times. I have failed at the part of inference sometimes.

My first time in college, I saw lots of well-dressed pretty women wearing safety pins that had been decorated with variously colored short ribbons that seemed to match their clothes. I made a color-coordinated pin for each of my outfits and wore them until a woman who was offended that I would steal her sorority's colors dressed me down. I never again trusted what I saw to be appropriate.

Still, I watched and learned.

I grew up with paper napkins. We kept them by our plates and picked them up to wipe our mouths. If we were eating something particularly messy, I would spread out the paper and tuck the tip into my shirt. The restaurants we went to growing up all provided paper napkins. Sometimes they gave us rectangular and thicker napkins than the Viva brand we used at home, but they were always paper. The first time

I used a cloth napkin was at prom, which was held at the Hotel du Pont, the nicest hotel in town. But I kept it on the table.

I was in my late twenties before I noticed people around me putting their napkins on their laps. This didn't make sense to me. The mess I make when I eat is on my face or on my shirt. I never get stains on my pants because the drips drop at the shelf on my chest. Why wouldn't I want the napkin closer?

I asked a friend when I first noticed the napkin in the lap, and she laughed at me, saying only white trash tuck their napkins in their shirts. A napkin on my lap still doesn't make sense to me, because after my friend laughed at me, I became afraid of asking about social class conventions.

Finally, at twenty-nine, I had my chance. My friend Nils presented artichokes to go with the baked chicken he'd just taken out of the oven.

"How about artichokes for our vegetable? Fresh from my garden."

I nodded and smiled, hoping to see artichoke prep firsthand, but knowing I would have to pretend that I already knew how to cook and eat it.

"You start the chokes while I get the chicken out of the oven?"

"No, I'll take the bird out. It'll only be a minute." I didn't even want to touch the artichokes because they looked painful to handle.

He palmed the blooms and told me a story about getting kicked out of the kitchen of his navy battleship because the cook thought he got in the way.

So the leaves don't hurt, I thought.

"He also didn't want me to get my officer's uniform dirty."

"I don't want you to stain your clothes either. That's why I'm dealing with the dirty bird!"

As I tented the chicken with foil, I watched him cut off most of the stem and place the thistles into a steamer. The pot's top teetered on the tallest one, so he balanced it on one edge.

"Have you ever had artichokes cooked any other way?" I asked.

"Hearts in brine, but those are steamed too. Have you?"

"Oh, I thought since you'd traveled the world in the navy, you'd have seen some unusual things." I moved to the kitchen table and started folding napkins that he'd taken out of the dryer a few minutes before into rectangles, wanting to keep myself occupied so he wouldn't ask me to check on the vegetable. Or ask me to turn the fabric squares into a bird.

"I've seen lots of strange things. Nothing with an artichoke. I think there's only one way to cook and eat an artichoke. To eat any thistle."

After carving the chicken, he placed one bloom on each of our plates, and a bowl of what looked like mayonnaise between us. The green globe smelled most like steamed spinach. He ate his chicken before picking at his vegetable.

Then he plucked off each leaf, one by one, dipped it into the sauce he called "broccolati," which I now know to be aioli—mayo with lemon and garlic—and scraped the tender flesh off each leaf with his teeth.

I followed his lead until I got to a hairy blob. I didn't know what to do, so I took my napkin off my lap and placed it onto the table, which I'd learned the year before was the signal that you are done with your meal.

"You're not going to eat the heart? That's the best part!"

I wanted to eat the heart, but I didn't want to embarrass myself by not knowing what to do with the hairs.

"No, I'm full. You go ahead if you want."

Nils scraped the hairy ball out of his artichoke heart with a spoon, being careful to get every fiber but none of the vegetable's center, cut the heart in four, and ate them without any aioli. While he scraped at mine, I asked him how he learned to eat an artichoke.

"I don't remember. My mother cooked them for us, and I suppose I learned from her."

These days, the Internet and YouTube how-to videos can teach me just about anything. I can, for instance, mimic my partner's very privileged family when we go to very fine restaurants to celebrate a birthday or anniversary without worrying that I'll be judged as white trash. I'll use the tiny spoon to sprinkle salt on my dinner like everyone else at the table, and will learn later about why petite bowls and spoons are better than a saltshaker, with the poet Pablo Neruda's tenderhearted warrior always on my mind.

I've used online video searches to learn how to make a lamb bal-samic reduction, how to sprinkle *fleur de sel* as a finishing salt on a deli-cate endive salad, and how to slice open a mango, all things my mother would find too strange for her liking.

Though I'm sure she'll like that I now keep a small jar of bacon fat in my freezer because in the twenty-some years I've been out of her house, I've not found a better fat in which to fry an egg. The next time I see her, I'll make a dip with mayonnaise, crème fraîche (telling her it is sour cream), and white truffle oil (telling her it is made from mush-rooms), and I'll teach Mom how to eat an artichoke.

Here's How to Drive the Poor Crazy

MICHAELANN BEWSEE

It's raining and I'm driving home from the organization I helped start, Arise for Social Justice, with a knot in my stomach because I've just found out Legal Services is drastically cutting services, when suddenly my windshield wipers stop working—just freeze in place.

"Jesus H. Christ," I say to myself. The wipers were intermittent (no pun intended) throughout the winter but had behaved really well the last two months, and I'd just totally forgotten I can't count on them. This reminds me that I've got to stop and pick up power-steering fluid because I have a leak in the system, which will cost about $400 to repair, and I know I've poured at least that much in fluid into my car over the last six months but at least it was only a few bucks at a time. But that's what being poor is all about, right?—paying twice as much because you can't afford to pay once.

I'm a sixty-one-year-old white woman who's about to lose her job with another organization (budget cuts) but feeling somewhat OK about it emotionally because it means I can spend more time at Arise, although how I'm going to get by I just don't know. However, this doesn't feel very different from what my life has been so far; having had a halfway-decent job for two years seems like a fluke.

Some days I look around at people and everyone seems so beautiful and alive, yet other days everyone seems so full of pain. I glance at the high school girl on the corner, screaming and crying into her cell phone, lest she walk unseeing into the path of my car. I drive by an old man in a motorized wheelchair with a plastic bag draped around his shoulders to protect him from the rain. I think about the ten-year-old girl I knew who grew up to be an exotic dancer and who was shot in the buttocks last night at the strip club where she works.

"Maybe today's a good day to write this thing about class," I think. I'd wanted to write this reasoned analysis—maybe to show poor people can think?—but it seems as if only strong emotion is going to get me moving.

I arrive home to my incredibly affordable tenement that I am so incredibly lucky to have lived in for the last two years—the first time in thirty years I've lived alone! Six rooms. A porch. Scratched hardwood floors. Wicker and bamboo furniture that I have lovingly collected secondhand through the years. And my thousands of books.

Illness and books shielded me from class awareness for many years when I was a child. I had rheumatic fever, couldn't go to school, couldn't do much of anything, in fact—but I *could* read, and I read everything in my working-class parents' house. I spent most of my real life in Arabia, China, Ireland, Scotland, and Sherwood Forest. I also had a seat at the Algonquin Round Table, thanks to poetry by Dorothy Parker, humor by Robert Benchley, and plays by George S. Kaufman. By age ten I'd also read the 1945 edition of Emily Post's *Etiquette* cover to cover more than once. I could hardly wait for the time when I was well and then could participate in the heady, creative, and yet somehow genteel world of the intellectual.

I had no idea money had anything to do with it.

As I grew older, I did become more aware of where my family stood in class rankings. I knew my parents struggled with bills, many of them related to my illness, but we never seemed exactly poor. Both of my parents would have said we were going somewhere, moving up from their own parents' situations.

Yet class warfare reigned within my own family. My mother's mother was lace-curtain Irish Catholic, widowed early by a Protestant who'd been disowned by his upper-class family for marrying beneath him. She worked in a laundry for much of her life and then was housekeeper for a priest until he died, but she always managed to convey she was meant for better things.

My father's mother was mostly Norwegian, grew up on a farm, had a fourth-grade education, and married a French Indian carpenter who became a bootlegger during the Depression and supported a large extended family on his illegal earnings.

The Irish side of my family looked down on the French side. I secretly sympathized with the French and wished I'd known my grandfather, who, I was told, also played minor league baseball and danced ballroom exquisitely well.

At seventeen, at the cusp of the post-Beat and counterculture eras, I fell in love with a black intellectual artist twice my age who worked at a bookstore where I hung out. He also happened to be bisexual and a drinker. When our relationship ended, I was pregnant.

Fast forward through my desperate flight from my parents' stifling home with my daughter, her abduction by my parents, the lawyer who told me that I, as a single mother, stood no chance of custody against a "middle-class, two-parent family." I wound up living in Cambridge, waitressing, being a hippy, and acting as a foot soldier against the war in Vietnam.

One night, after a major demonstration, I was hanging out with two boys from Harvard when one of them, moved by the honesty of LSD, said to me, "You know, you are always going to be different from us."

"Really?" I said. "Why?"

"Because we'll have gone to college and you won't have." There was no malice in his statement. He was just telling the truth. I'd just never heard it before.

There were two kinds of hippies in Cambridge those days—the college kids and the townies. I spent the night with my townie friend, the great love of my life, who is probably dead from drugs or violence or locked up for the rest of his life; I only know I have been unable to find him.

I used to hitch back and forth to the Cape on weekends, and one day I was picked up by an older man who was a poet, so we had much to talk about. I wound up staying at his understated home in Truro, and he invited me to come visit him at his Beacon Hill townhouse. Only on my first visit did I realize he must have money, and at first he seemed to live in exactly the world I wanted to live in—house packed with books, literary and progressive friends—but after a while I felt like I was on display as this quirky, smart, pretty little thing he'd snatched from the streets. I began to feel smothered by the relationship, didn't much care for him sexually, and got tired of his looking at me sideways to watch my reactions to the situations he put me in. I decided that the next time I saw him, I was going to tell him I wanted to break it off.

I was invited to his house two days before Christmas, prepared to let him know it was over *before* the obligatory sex. He was a bright guy, and I think he'd sensed the cooling in our relationship. After dinner he handed me an envelope as a Christmas present and told me not to open it until I got home, and then he conveniently went out for wine, so of course I peeked and it was a check for $500! Immediately my mind jumped to the Christmas presents I could buy for my daughter—I sure didn't have much yet—and I thought about my housemates: the incessantly cheerful runaway Judy, who was escaping sexual abuse at home, skinny street flutist Bernard, born twenty years too late, and Big Dave, an unemployed divorced dad that I knew had been obsessing over his own kids' Christmas. We'd have money for the holidays!

Wow. This guy just gave me $500. Am I really going to take the money and run? Didn't it only seem *fair* I'd sleep with him one last time? So I did. And the next day, I couldn't cash the check! I didn't have a bank account, I didn't have a driver's license, and I had to call him up and ask for help getting it cashed. Then I went home, distributed the money, and went out shopping Christmas Eve for my daughter.

I found out later he'd expected me to "do something" with the money—maybe rent a storefront and sell the jewelry I made. But of course I hadn't. It was the first time in that free-love era when I'd felt like a whore. I got some satisfaction, at least, out of knowing I was a better poet.

Fast forward through my own addiction, the years of getting centered in Providence, meeting and (sort of) marrying my second daughter's father, a Brown student, our years of homesteading in Maine, his nervous breakdown, and my return to my hometown Springfield, pregnant and alone. I was almost thirty, and I applied for welfare. I lived for a year in a fourth-floor flat with my daughter and one day answered an ad from a woman looking for three or four women to share a house. I met her, liked her, we found two other women, and then we found an old Victorian in a mostly black neighborhood. I never could have guessed I would live there for the next thirty years.

The other women were all professionals, and with a few exceptions, they turned over rather quickly, moving to Amherst or Northampton where they were more comfortable, to be gradually replaced by family members (my older daughter! Finally!) and friends in need. One of the last of the original to leave was a woman who was going to move as soon as she replaced her college-era car, now coming to the end of its life.

"Guess what I did?" she said one night. "I found a solution to my car situation!"

"What did you do?"

"I took it down to the Puerto Rican section and left it unlocked with the keys in the car. You know it won't last long, and then I can report it as stolen."

"Wait a minute—somebody could get arrested over this. Some kid who's never stolen anything before could see your car and be tempted, and then get busted. You're setting somebody up!"

"Well," she huffed, "if someone's going to be a thief then they will be—doesn't matter if it's my car or some other."

God, how I hated her.

Life rolled on. On my landlord's suggestion, I and other tenants in his properties worked to form a housing co-op only to find out, after three years, that he'd put second mortgages on all our homes and the project wasn't financially viable. (He was a "rob Peter to pay Paul" sort of guy.) One day there was a knock at the door and four suited white men announced my house was being auctioned off. A Georgia mortgage company put in the only bid, and its representative said his company would be in touch. I never heard another word from them, and for the next ten years I paid not one penny of rent to anybody, allowing me, when my political work took off full time, to get by on very little money. How I loved that house, especially its huge backyard where I gardened year after year. But it was like living in limbo.

I started doing a little housecleaning on the side. I especially hated cleaning the absolutely spotless homes of the owning class in Longmeadow. Once an owner wandered through the kitchen where, on her instructions, I was washing the floor on my hands and knees with a sponge. She smiled brightly and said, "No rest for the wicked, huh?" In other words, I was on my knees in her kitchen because I deserved to be.

I joined the local peace coalition to work on the nuclear freeze and was cultivated by a man who later turned out to be looking for recruits for the Communist Labor Party. I already knew about poverty, but I was about to find out *why*. I started going to small meetings at his house, where I read and discussed the classics. I didn't understand the party, though, or why everything had to be so secret, or why only I could take the party paper down to the factory gates. It seems everyone else had too much to lose to be publicly identified with the party.

I called my mother one day to check in. She was now a widow, chronically ill, and barely keeping a household together with my brother and sister still at home. She told me she had been turned down for fuel assistance because her annual income put her seven dollars over the limit. Suddenly everything came together. I sat down and wrote the following poem. Within three months I had resigned from the party and met the three women with whom I would form the poor people's rights organization, Arise for Social Justice.

FIRST YOU CREATE THE POOR THEN YOU CREATE A WAY TO HELP THEM

Here's how to drive the poor crazy:
tell us it's not charity;
make us beg for it.
Don't be available by phone.
Make us wait in the office
until we discover
you're gone for the day.
Put us in lines in the cold
where we're ashamed to complain to each other.
Close the factories, open the soup kitchens.

Tell us there's nothing you can do.
Bury us in forms and file numbers.
Lose our paperwork.
Teach us to work in obsolete fields.
Offer us plastic for unheated apartments.

Shame our children for having bad teeth
and for wearing sneakers in January.
Underpay the parents
and give the kids free lunch.
Close the schools, open the training centers.

Make sure the checks are late,
especially before Christmas.
Refuse to cash our checks
for lack of sufficient balance.
Jack up the prices in our neighborhood.
Give us medicine
medicaid won't pay for.
Give us vouchers
no one will accept.
Take out the pay phones.
Make the bus lines end nowhere.
Raise the rents and open the shelters.

Here's how to bring on your own downfall:
get us together in the same waiting room
once too often.
Make the size of the lie greater
so our last illusions are destroyed.
Put more of us in jail.
Keep eliminating options.
Send our children home smaller
one more time.
Look away for a moment.

Thirty years later, I have few regrets. I wish I could have done more to help my mother and daughters financially. I wish life wasn't so hard sometimes. And occasionally I still wish for the cerebral world of my childhood. But if I can't have it all, then I still choose to ally myself with other poor people. I have found it too painful to spend much time outside my own class, where the judgmentalness of others toward the poor makes me want to put up my fists.

I love the work that I've done with my hands, the tangible accomplishments of assembling a product or harvesting a crop. I love the political work that's shaped me—flipping pancakes at a Black Panther Free Breakfast program, writing for a women's paper, hitting the streets with flyers that say, We have rights, we matter, our lives are important.

I would like to tell you the whole story of poor people, but telling you about my own life will have to do.

Red Datsun Security

KAREN SPECTOR

The driver's seat of my red Datsun wasn't properly bolted to the car floor. I think there were four points at which the seat had once been firmly secured to the car body, back when it was a new, brightly painted auto on the lot, but now only one bolt managed to hang on. The result was a mixture of rocking and swiveling that made for perilous driving, though also for freedom in reaching into the back seat for a sweater or into the glove compartment for some gum, and all with the seat belt still firmly attached.

I sat at the red light on the corner of Thirty-Fourth Street and Archer Road in my Datsun, feeling jubilant and safe. But why did I feel this way? After all, my forehead was still stinging from the blow received from the windshield when I braked too quickly for the light and my unhinged seat launched me forward. So why was I feeling secure and happy? I looked down Thirty-Fourth Street to where Fred, my "older" boyfriend, lived and then up at the sky. Like Louise Mallard in Kate Chopin's "Story of an Hour," I felt the answer to my question "creeping out of the sky," gathering in the humid air, and pushing itself toward me. A realization. An illumination. I said it out loud: "Free, free, free!" and then my face turned hot with shame.

My sister Jo was the original owner of the Datsun. As a down payment, she used the $3,000 my mom squirreled away for her from the government survivor benefits we received after my dad died.

Like my sister, my brother Rick used his $3,000 to buy a car when he turned eighteen. Always the odd one out, I took my life savings and went off to the University of Florida. A car, or a college education?

In a beautiful twist, my sister's Datsun became my college graduation gift from my whole family. Rick agreed to sell Jo his old car cheaply, so Jo gave the Datsun to my mom and stepfather to fix up for me. They took it in for some new tires and a tune-up, wrapped it in a bow, and handed it over to me as I headed back to Gainesville to pursue my master's degree. It was already on its way out; in fact, in two year's time I would pay a scrap dealer in Cranston, Rhode Island, one hundred dollars to tow it from the street where it finally breathed its last. But the Datsun was a welcomed gift, an unexpected luxury.

Throughout my undergrad years my only wheels had been those of city buses or a bicycle. I lived far from campus—cheaper that way— and worked nearly full time at Captain D's restaurant and later at the Cinema Drafthouse—turned out that $3,000 isn't really enough to buy a college education. I got off of work sometimes well after midnight when the buses were already down for the night, so except for the occasional kindness of a coworker who could throw my bike in his trunk, I rode my bike to and from work every night, miles down the unlit Archer Road from Thirty-Fourth Street to Tower Road. This was always a dangerous trip, fraught with close calls with tipsy or ticked-off drivers who seemed to view the presence of a young woman biking down an unlit road at midnight a nuisance.

When I started dating Fred near the end of my junior year, my midnight biking trips ended. Fred was five years older than I, already graduated with his master's degree, and working in a real job. He began dropping me off and picking me up from work. I liked him, and I was grateful to him. I lived so far out, it was just easier, he said, to stay at his place. I didn't have sex with him for months, but then he planned a trip to the Cayman Islands and invited me along. I had never been out of the country before. On this trip, I consented to sex, of course. When we returned to Gainesville, he continued picking me up from work in the evening, so spending nights with him (and all that entailed) was just part of our relationship.

It wasn't until I got my Datsun and was idling at the red light on the corner of Thirty-Fourth Street and Archer Road that it came to me from the sky, that it gathered in the humid air, and pressed into me with a heat of a shameful revelation: I was free. The Datsun made Fred less essential. I thought, "I don't need Fred anymore. I will be secure without him." I pushed it out of my mind, and shortly thereafter I pushed Fred out of my life.

It wasn't until my son Zach turned seventeen that I revisited this story, prompted by a disagreement between my husband and me about buying Zach a car. It wasn't the best time to buy a car; that much was true. We had just moved from Ohio so I could start a new position at the University of Alabama, my husband lost his job, and we had been draining our 401(k) to make ends meet. The big plus of taking the Alabama job was that college tuition was low, and as a professor I could get my family half off. Half off low tuition was a big selling point.

"You didn't have a car until after your undergrad, and you turned out okay," my husband argued. And it was then that I rocked back in my seat at the memory from twenty years earlier.

"If it takes our last dime, we will buy him a car." And we did buy Zach a used convertible with a driver's seat securely bolted to the floor. I smiled jubilantly as I drove it home from the dealership, and at a red light, with car top down, I mused: Who was I that I could afford to buy my son a car? That I had savings to live on? My people didn't go to college, have savings, or even know if the stock market rose or fell.

Security and freedom have been in tension for me my whole life, shifting targets never primarily about money, but about money and access nonetheless. In high school, it was about being the first in the family to go to college (instead of going directly to work); in college, it was about finding ways to get to and from work safely (so I could pay for college and the easier life it would lead to); and at this moment in time, though I'm now middle class, it is about making the decisions necessary to provide my oldest child with a college education *and* a car, so he will be more free than I was, so that he will be able to live without bending his will to someone else's unless he freely chooses to.

A Box from My Grandfather

JANET CASEY

In my first year of college, my grandfather sent me a large cardboard box filled with unrelated odds and ends that he somehow thought I needed, or perhaps wanted. This assortment, I perceived immediately, was intended to help me fit in, to make me feel like a genuine college student; the only problem was that my grandfather had no idea what sorts of things might actually accomplish those goals. To me, then, his efforts seemed ill-conceived and embarrassing—reminders of a past from which I was already trying to distance myself.

It was about halfway through my first semester, and I was attending a liberal arts college an hour from my home. My grandfather made it clear that he wanted to visit me, and in particular that he wanted to see my dorm room. Because a bout with cancer had robbed him of clear speech, he preferred to visit in the middle of a weekday morning, when most students would be in class and he would be less likely to feel pressured to converse. He was driven out to the college by my father, and their "visit" lasted no more than five minutes. Pop, as we called my grandfather, entered my room, hugged me, and then looked around slowly and carefully. Almost nothing was said. Then, abruptly, he indicated to my father that he was ready to go home. That was it. They headed to the car, and I went to class, annoyed by what seemed to me a pointless intrusion into my newfound world.

Two weeks later the box arrived, clarifying my grandfather's purpose in making that visit. In the space of those five minutes, he had assessed my roommate's visible belongings, perceived mine to be lacking, and made mental note of items that might close the gap. I learned later that he had handed my mother some money and a list, assuming that she would shop for him (as she always had) and take care of the shipping. This stark act was his way of coping with the uncertainties raised by a granddaughter who made the bold move of not just attending college, but of *going away*.

I recall my amusement as I unwrapped from the box an extendable reading lamp that could be attached to a bed—a near replica of that belonging to my roommate, who was the daughter of a dentist and who seemed to have arrived at college with boxes and boxes of her own. My grandfather never suspected that I found my roommate's stuff, on the whole, to be over the top in a new-student-at-college kind of way, excessive, adolescent, and fastidious. The lamp, I thought ruefully, was not my kind of thing. Besides, if I wanted to fit in with the privileged students all around me, what I really needed was much more than a lamp: I needed more and better clothing, perhaps a car, and—dare I say it?—spring break excursions to Florida. Those were the things everyone else seemed to have, and those were the things I thought I wanted. But how would a sixty-eight-year-old truck driver with an eighth-grade education know that?

In retrospect, I'm grieved by my self-absorbed, eighteen-year-old self, the one who loved her grandfather but found him extraneous to the new life unfolding before her. In those college years my entire family seemed to me to be parochial and uninformed. We were hardly poor; on the contrary, we were solidly situated in a working-class neighborhood in the very house my mother had grown up in, and my father's job was reliable enough to allow my mother to stay out of the workforce for most of my growing-up years. But, significantly, I was the first in the family to attend college. My father had plowed doggedly through several years of night school but never earned a degree; I was the first to enroll full time (the only one to live away for the duration), and the first to finish. Moreover, my course of study marked me early on as different: though my BA gratified my parents, my double major in English and music caused them some unease and sharply differentiated me from my siblings, who entered preprofessional pro-grams that were perceived to be "useful" in that they led to obvious employment opportunities. In contrast, I kept attending school, even-tually earning a PhD, becoming a professor of American literature, and moving very far, culturally speaking, from where I had come from.

But college was where it all started, where I began to perceive for the first time that the world was much larger, much more complex, and far more interesting than I had previously realized. And on an educa-tional level, I loved every minute of it; I still consider it the most intel-lectually exciting and expansive time of my life. Yet my grandfather's box served to remind me that a huge gulf was opening between me and my family, even as I failed to assimilate fully into the campus culture surrounding me. Having scraped together sufficient loans, grants, and jobs (not to mention the sacrifices my parents made) to attend a private college, I discovered, too late, that in some sense I would never really feel that I belonged there.

Indeed, I felt acutely different from my classmates, who were com-fortable in art museums and bookstores, and for whom educated adults and wide-ranging dinner conversation were commonplace. In contrast, I had never seen an art film, never attended a professional music or dance performance, never taken an airplane. And I learned quickly that others would laugh at my class-related gaffes, such as my innocent assumptions that the cars in the parking lot belonged wholly to staff and faculty, or that all the students, like me, had a campus job (or two). I tried not to reveal that I was dazzled by the choices in the dining hall, awed by the sports facilities, genuinely fond of the plush chairs in secret corners of the library; my college campus was the loveliest place I had ever lived. I even rejoiced in my shared dorm room—bigger than the room at home that I shared with my sister, and with my very own closet!

What strikes me now, however, is that my grandfather understood in some vague way that these material differences would matter, and he tried to alleviate them. In my later years, his box has seemed to me a precious thing, a lifeline thrown haphazardly to a child who seemed in some way needy, from a grandfather who could not quite interpret the need but who wanted to provide in whatever way he could. I am deeply touched, now, by that box and what it signified. And when I remember my grandfather, who died at the very end of my freshman year, I have a deeper understanding of his concern for me, and of his enormous pride that I was in college at all. I regret that I didn't save that box; I don't even recall everything that was in it. But I did save the ugly, clunky lamp—attached, at one point, to the bed of my son, who has benefited from the education of his parents in ways he will never fully understand.

Even more important is my awareness, late in coming, that the background that seemed so humiliating in those days can be a source of strength and self-respect. To be sure, I have learned to speak a new language, an educated language that my family does not share or even understand; yet the working-class culture I came from is also a part of me, by far the most formative piece of all. And if I impart anything to those first-generation college students who occasionally come my way, it's that such a background can give them a fuller perspective of the world, a richer range of experiences to draw on, a more compassionate stance in relation to abstract notions of *ability*, *merit*, and *need*. My gift to them—my box, as it were—consists not of material things but of empathy, recognition, sensitivity, pep talks. In reaching out to them as a self-identified member of the working classes, I strive to encourage them in whatever ways I can, misguided and clumsy though my efforts sometimes are.

My grandfather, I think, would understand.

Vacuum Cleaner Truth

SIERRA FLEENOR

"Okay. If you finish vacuuming before I finish cleaning the bathroom, you can watch TV while I dust. If I finish first, I get to watch TV while you dust," my older sister said, coaxing me into a bet. I tried to calculate whether or not I could push the heavy vacuum quickly enough to beat her bathtub scrubbing.

"Deal," I replied with defiance.

"On your mark. Get set. Go!" she called.

My mom had left to pick up some more cleaning supplies and the list of condominiums we would need to clean that day, so my sister and I seized the opportunity to play. I heaved the cumbersome machine to and fro in the living room, barely able to see around it. I kept hoping I would win, longing to watch television on a color set for a change. I peered into the bathroom to spy on my sister scouring the sink in a fury. If I could maneuver my way around the dining table deftly, I just might finish first.

"*Done!*" I screamed in glee. "I did it. I beat you. I'm done!"

Ecstatic at the work my eight-year-old hands had accomplished, I was too busy celebrating and locating the best channel for cartoons to really think about how different my summers were from those enjoyed by my peers. I enjoyed my summers just as much, and the games I played with a vacuum were not really that different from those my friends played with a jump rope. The work (and play) I did alongside my mother and sister supported our family. We needed all the help we could muster to clean these vacation homes that remained unoccupied seven months of the year in our small ski town. We were able to work more quickly when we were together, six hands better than two, even if a pair of those hands were smaller.

What I did not realize then was that my childhood games highlighted the socioeconomic class difference between me and my peers. This did not dawn on me as a child and evaded me up until I entered college. In fact, I do not think I had ever heard the term "socioeconomic class" before the spring of my first year of undergraduate study. I do not blame my high school teachers. How were they supposed to broach the topic with a classroom full of students, most of whose parents had never been to college, and most of whom would never attend college either? College-bound students stood out. We almost rose above our peers, having attention constantly poured on us by teachers and guidance counselors. Anyone looking at us—outstanding students, involved in extracurriculars, attentive, and bright—would have simply seen hardworking children who had the future laid before them. And, in most cases, they were right. But in my case, they missed the mark.

I had no idea what college meant. I knew I was supposed to go and that I should try to go to a good school because I had done well on the ACT. My parents did not really know how to encourage me. My father had a trade degree and opened his own business as a farrier, or horseshoer. My mother was a homemaker and had received her GED. Their parents were equally uneducated. I was the first of my kind, even outachieving my older sister by being the first to face the difficulty of college admissions. With some amazing guidance and a good deal of luck, I found a school—or it found me—and I eagerly enrolled, bright-eyed and bushy-tailed.

College was not easy for me, though. I spent two and a half years in extreme denial of my background. I suddenly found myself surrounded by students from upper-middle-class America. In a country where the very idea of social class (and its hereditary advantages or disadvantages) stands against our truest ideal—the American dream—I desired desperately to belong. Academically, I was able to get along. I was by no means as well prepared for college as my peers, but I worked hard and approached my studies creatively. Outside the classroom, I tried to fit in with my peers by adopting their habits and language. I stopped talking about "mutton bustin'" and my experiences as a housekeeper or the daughter of a horse-shoer. I stopped saying "ain't" and using idioms like "keep on with the keepin' on." I started eating out more, and quickly put myself in debt. I did my best to appear like any other student, but my heart sank every time I saw the woman who cleaned the common areas of our dorm.

I do not remember her name. I do not even remember what she looked like. However, the image of her stooped over a toilet, scrubbing the porcelain throne of the privileged, remains burned upon my brain. I can clearly see her uniform and the cart she pushed full of cleaning supplies. I cannot remember her name because I never spoke with her. While other students would ask her about her weekend, I avoided her. I was embarrassed by her presence, but I was more embarrassed by my own presence. Her story was my story to some degree. We had both cleaned the living spaces of strangers. We both knew which cleaning supplies best removed mildew, rust, or soap scum. We were both working class. I could not face that fact, and I sought to escape her. I turned away from her and away from myself.

A year later, I sat in class listening to my professor. He was telling us about when he lived in inner-city Chicago and the woman he was dating at the time. They had gone grocery shopping, and she had pulled out food stamps with which to buy that night's dinner. He talked about this girlfriend with ease, as he spoke about most things. Our relaxed interactions were marked by joking and casual conversation, so I thought little of my playful banter, asking, "Does your wife know about this girlfriend?" He turned to look at me. "My wife is from humble roots and would never judge someone for using food stamps." I sat, mouth agape. "Professor Dawson, neither would I. That's . . . that's . . . not what I meant." "Yes it is, Sierra." I felt my stomach sink and my ears turn red. "I grew up on welfare. I have held food stamps and looked the clerk in the face as he took them from me," I said, the answer flying from my mouth.

At the time, I thought he was wrong. I thought he had misjudged me. Even he thought he was wrong and apologized to me later. I see now, though, that he was right. By not speaking up, by not talking about my socioeconomic class background, I was judging those who used food stamps. I was judging the woman who cleaned my dorm. I judged my parents—not allowing them to meet my new peers. I judged my peers, assuming they would think I was less than them because of how I was raised. By trying to control the effect socioeconomic class had on my life, I let my fear of talking about class control everything.

Now as I sit here writing, I understand. This is a part of me—a large part. The only way to escape my shame and to break the cycle is to talk about my life. I have to speak up, so I will tell my story.

When my mother, my sole guardian, was imprisoned, I changed homes, moving in with a middle-class family. I left the life I had known as a young girl. The only physical labor I engaged in while I lived there was helping to build a fence, something I had once done in addition to my housekeeping work when I was younger. I found the routine I knew well as a child of moving from room to room, racing my sister to see who could finish her task quicker, was not commonplace. I started to question my childhood. I wanted to know what the part-time residents of these homes had done to deserve so much more than my family. I wanted to know who else had lived in trailers like me, who had reduced cost for school meals, and whose parents did not go to college and worked with their hands, not to mention their backs, knees, and elbows. I started my lifelong quest to investigate socioeconomic class then and there. I did not know the journey I was embarking on. Nor did I sense that I would one day hide the work my family had done together. I do not think I realized then that I could ever be ashamed of what made me so proud at the time. I spent time with my family. My parents loved me. I played games. I knew that with hard work I could accomplish many things. I was so proud of who my parents had raised me to be. And while the journey has included twists and turns I never could have predicted, I have found my way back to myself. I remember what it means to be a little redheaded girl playing vacuum-cleaner games with her sister. And, I am proud.

I Am Working Class

MICHELLE M. TOKARCZYK

If I ask myself when I first became aware of class or, specifically, of the class to which I belonged, I realize that I had not one epiphany, but rather several. The reality of my working-class childhood would crystallize, only to be forgotten (or repressed) again. I could not hold on to an identity as someone who grew up in the working class until I could talk and write about my experiences with people from the working class.

MY CHILDHOOD MEMORIES are marked with recollections of my family's economic struggle. During my early childhood my father was a "parkie"; he did basic maintenance in a New York City park. My mom stayed home with my sister and me; money was always tight. In my school's Christmas play, my first-grade class was singing songs by the then popular Alvin and the Chipmunks. All of us students were told to get harmonicas. I could not bring myself to ask my mother to buy me something she had not already decided was an absolute necessity. Each time that our class practiced for the play, I told my teacher I'd ask my mother for a harmonica, and each day I resolved to do so. But I couldn't.

I arrived for the performance without a harmonica; my exasperated teacher gave me and me alone a tambourine, which I hit without rhythm or enthusiasm. Unconcerned with clothing, I was unaware that my parents had bought me a new dress from the main floor of Alexander's—a rare departure from their basement shopping, which would later become rummage-sale shopping. "Why didn't you have a harmonica?" my bewildered and probably shamed father asked me gently when he met me in my classroom after the show. "They're so expensive," I said quietly, head down.

WHEN I WAS NINE YEARS OLD my mother looked out our apartment window and saw two boys fighting with baseball bats. The fights among boys increased, and sometimes knives were drawn. Alarmed, my parents joined the white flight from the Bronx and bought a fixer-upper house in a quiet area of Queens. The house my parents bought had only five small rooms and a minimal bathroom that had to be completely remodeled. Because the property was below the street level, the house looked far smaller than it was—as though it were only about ten feet from base to roof.

I was a very shy child, and it took me awhile to make friends, but in time I found that two classmates lived on the half-mile route I walked to school. Edna, Kara, and I became fast friends, going to school and standing together in line before the nuns marched us into the school. Because Kara and Edna lived closer to the school than I, they had not seen my house. One day on the way home we all decided that I'd show them my house (just the outside—no one came inside the house, which was still under renovation). When we arrived at my home, Kara burst into laughter. "It's so small! I've never seen such a small house! It's a good thing you're all small people." I said nothing. What could I say? It was a really small house.

A day or two later, Edna approached me, looking very serious, "I think Kara was very mean in laughing about your house." I knew that Edna wanted to make me feel better, but she made me feel worse.

My father, who had grown up in apartments and had barely known how to wield a hammer before moving to Queens, took pride in his construction efforts. He put up walls, put in insulation, plastered, and painted inside and out. Much of the work was jury-rigged, but it was his work, nonetheless. My mother, far more sensitive to other people's opinions, was constantly shamed by the house. My sister and I got head lice in what was undoubtedly a school outbreak. (Although no one talked about lice, there were telltale signs of their presence in the rash of boys' crew cuts and girls' shoulder-length hair trimmed to bobs.) Mom insisted my father look for delousing shampoos in drugstores in neighboring areas where no one could possibly recognize us. If our neighbors learned of our infestation, she lamented, they'd be certain that we were "white trash."

A few years later my father made top pay at his job as a toll collector on the Whitestone Bridge (a big step up from "parkie," though Dad always missed working outdoors). My parents looked for a bigger, better house in the same locale so that my sister and I would not have to travel to attend our Catholic high school. No one who could qualify for any kind of mortgage was interested in our home. Mom and Dad eventually made a deal with someone we'd now call a sub-prime borrower. They held the mortgage and for many years received minimal payments.

About a week before the move I wrote a letter to my grade-school friend Edna, who was now attending a different high school and whom I rarely saw. In what I remember as typical fifteen-year-old fashion, I wrote about several new and exciting things—the cute male teachers in my all-girls high school, the classes I was taking, the new house my family had bought, and our mutual friends' activities. Edna responded with a short note saying that she was very happy to hear that my family was moving to a bigger house. I put her note in the bottom of a drawer, feeling stunned by her preoccupation with our small house and relieved that I rarely saw her.

MY PROCESS OF CHOOSING MY UNDERGRADUATE COLLEGE was distinctly different from that of middle- and upper-middle-class students today, who spend many hours preparing for SAT exams, visiting potential schools, and crafting admission essays. I knew that I would go to one of the City of New York University campuses. So did all of my friends in my all-girls Catholic high school. (Later, a boyfriend from an all-boys Catholic high school told me that his classmates were much more discriminating—as were their families.) The only different touch in my college choice was that rather than pick Queens College, as the vast majority of my classmates did, I chose Herbert Lehman College. I'd gone through grammar and high school with many of the same students and had grown tired of them, especially of their conservative political views. The quintessential college experience of living on campus held no appeal; I'd waited for years to have my own room, and I didn't want to relinquish that. However, I wanted a college with a campus, and the second logical choice, Hunter College, had none. I continued to harbor some fondness for the Bronx, so I chose Lehman College.

During one of my sociology classes we were asked to list ten ways to complete the statement, "I am . . ." I can't remember many of the terms I wrote, but one was "middle class." Years later I would wonder why I wrote those words. Many of my friends in the Bronx rented rather than owned their homes. Did I believe my family's home ownership—or, as I knew even then, my parents' possession of a mortgage they constantly struggled to pay—gave me entrée to the middle class? Had I forgotten the harmonica, the friend's mockery, my mother's shame? Had I erased them?

WHATEVER ERASURE or story of upward mobility I'd managed in my undergraduate years quickly evaporated when I graduated and applied for doctoral programs in English. Now I was immersed in a real application process, and with it the construction of my identity as a scholar.

When the application for Columbia University arrived, I'd just moved out of my parents' home to a small shared apartment near Lehman College, where I found work via a government-sponsored program for unemployed liberal arts graduates. I didn't have a typewriter, but I reasoned that the Admissions Committee must understand that not everyone has such things. My personal statement was drafted by hand and, when finished, neatly printed on the official application. The first sentence began, "I was born to a working-class family." In retrospect, I realize there were many flaws in my application and in my college transcript. However, when I got the rejection letter, all I could see was the application's first line.

IF SOMEONE HAD MENTIONED THE PHRASE "working-class solidarity" to me while I was growing up, I would have been bewildered. The times when I felt working class were the times when I felt alienated, ostracized, and distinctly different from my middle-class peers. Being middle class, in contrast, meant belonging; being middle class meant enjoying the rewards of life in America and the approval of those around you.

AFTER I FINISHED GRADUATE SCHOOL and was in the grueling process of applying for tenure-track jobs, I began to reflect on what had made my early years of graduate school so difficult. Why, I wondered, did I feel so arrogant in pursuing a doctorate? Why did I feel so unsure of my abilities and so certain that a gulf separated me from my peers who'd casually mention their parents' higher education experiences? They were expected to get advanced degrees. As a woman and a member of the working class, I was not.

I proposed a panel on working-class women in the academy that I thought might generate some interest among members of the Women's Caucus of the Modern Language Association of America. To my surprise, the panel was quickly accepted for the 1988 convention. To my greater surprise, the small room was packed, standing room only. People crowded the halls outside.

I think of that audience of working-class women who had, as I had, been living on the edges of academia. Each of us sitting, standing, speaking, taking notes, testifying that she was there and that she intended to stay and make her experience visible. Visible, first of all, to herself.

Hitting the Academic Class Ceiling

K. STRICKER

I grew up in a small, working-class town in rural South Dakota. Neither of my parents attained education beyond high school, yet they succeeded in making a reasonably comfortable life for me and my two siblings. My family had a small house and a relatively reliable used car. My dad had a decent job as a waterman for the city, which enabled my mother to stay home until my youngest brother started kindergarten.

My mother was a stay-at-home mom. I don't remember ever hearing a conversation about the importance of education. I knew good behavior in school was important, but as far as I can remember, I was not expected nor encouraged to excel. In my early elementary years I often performed below average. I have distinct memories of being assigned to the "brown" reading group for the slow readers in second grade and being sent down the hall to do remedial handwriting with the first-grade class. These experiences as a youngster led me to believe that I wasn't very smart.

I plodded through the rest of my elementary and middle-school years, doing the work that was interesting to me and not completing the work that wasn't. In fifth grade I was fortunate to have Mrs. Egan, who was a patient, caring teacher. While Mrs. Egan did many kind things for me, she made one simple statement that ended up being life-changing. Mrs. Egan told me, "Make sure you take debate in ninth grade. You are a good arguer." Looking back, I'm not even sure what the context of the statement was, but four years later I signed up for debate simply because Mrs. Egan said I should.

At my high school, the smart kids were generally encouraged to take debate, while the academically less talented were shuffled off to speech class. I would likely have been a victim of this de facto tracking if Mrs. Egan hadn't encouraged me to register for that debate class. A few weeks into the first semester of my ninth-grade year, I decided to compete at a debate tournament. It was after winning a few debate rounds against the smartest kids in the area that I had a significant "aha" moment. I remember thinking, "If I am winning debate rounds against smart kids, I might be smart as well." I tested my theory the next day by trying my best in all my classes. From that day on, I was nearly a straight A student.

I continued debating throughout high school with much success, twice qualifying for the national tournament and placing high at the state tournaments both my junior and senior year. During my senior year, I was involved in numerous conversations about the fancy colleges my friends on the debate team were applying to. One went to Harvard, another to Georgetown, and others were accepted into honors programs at various prestigious public and private institutions across the country. Looking back, it is interesting to me that I never even considered applying to any institution more than a few hours from my hometown. At the time, I didn't think it made much sense to go far away and spend a lot of money when I could get the same degree for less money.

When I think about the educational institutions I chose to attend, it is clear to me that social class played a significant role in my decisions. My worldview and my understanding of what was possible for me were limited by my family's expectations and my lack of exposure to life beyond my small town. After all, when I headed off to college, it was with the expectation that I would return to my hometown after completing my degree. Lacking the guidance of college-educated parents, I just didn't understand the importance of academic pedigree. On the other hand, my friends that went off to Harvard and Georgetown were the children of medical doctors. Their parents understood the opportunities that an Ivy League education could provide.

After graduating from college, I was hired to teach freshman debate at my old high school. Thinking back, it is not surprising that I went to college to become a high school teacher. Teaching was one of the few jobs in my hometown that I had been exposed to that required a college degree. During my first year of teaching I applied for and was awarded a $25,000 scholarship to pursue a master's degree at the institution of my choice. Despite the financial bounty, I applied only to the university closest to my home, fully unaware of the opportunities I was missing by not seeking out institutions based on academic reputation. I made the same mistake when I started my PhD program, matriculating at the first university that accepted me. At no time in my formal academic training did I consider the national reputation of the institutions I attended. My life experience told me that the schools that I went to were "good" schools, and I figured that good was good enough. I have since learned that it is common for kids from working-class families to choose their colleges based on cost and location rather than on academic reputation.

It was after accepting a teaching position at a small liberal arts university in the Midwest that I began to understand how my educational choices would limit my future opportunities. It was during my first year of teaching that one of my colleagues asked me, "Where do you see yourself professionally in five years?" I quickly responded, "I am happy here, I really love teaching here." My colleague replied, "Seriously? Don't you want to be at a Research One institution?" My naïveté was fully exposed when I had to ask her what she meant. Somehow, I had managed to complete two master's degrees, a PhD, and land a tenure-track position without fully understanding the entrenched hierarchy of higher education. I have since discovered, in academia, it does matter where you get your degree and who your mentors were. I have discovered that my lack of academic pedigree places real limits on the opportunities for professional advancement that are open to me. This is, for the most part, a reality that my middle-class colleagues don't confront.

At thirty-two years old I feel as though my head is firmly planted up against the class ceiling. The realization that I don't have the right pedigree has been painful, as has the understanding that in the eyes of many of the members of the academy, I am still a member of the "lower" class.

Blue-Collar Heart, Ivy League World

JENNIFER O'CONNOR DUFFY

As a professor of higher education, I derive my professional interest in upward mobility and the experiences of working-class women at elite academic institutions from my own experience as a working-class student at Amherst College. My maternal grand-parents, immigrants from Italy, never finished fifth grade; they were required to work to help pay for the family's expenses. As adults, they owned and operated an ice-cream store. Across the street, my paternal grandfather owned a gas station. My father grew up in low-income housing, otherwise known as the "projects." Although he was accepted to college, his parents did not have the funds for tuition. Instead, they gave him $1,000 as compensation. Thus, I was a first-generation college student on my father's side of the family.

My life story dances and mourns around the cyclical themes associated with classism: pride and embarrassment, resentment and longing, acceptance and rejection. As the daughter of a working-class family who lived in the poorer section of an upper-class town, I occupied a social world that was painted with contradictory and sometimes painful realities. My journey speaks to the dreams of a young girl hoping to escape the ignorance and financial difficulties of her childhood.

When I was eight years old, my family moved from a blue-collar neighborhood to an upper-class town. Prior to the move, my days were blissfully innocent as I biked around the neighborhood, visited the ice-cream truck nightly, and knew everyone's first name in the community. However, when my parents decided to move us to a "better" town with a "school system that was going to get us into a good college," my perceptions were drastically altered. I was initially excited by the move and filled with anticipation at the prospect of riding the school bus and being awed by the gigantic houses. But little did I know at the time that moving ten minutes away would profoundly affect who I was to become.

I vividly remember, in fifth grade, a surf-and-turf dinner at my friend Beth Smith's[1] house that was interrupted by my father's arrival in uniform (he needed to pick me up before his night shift started). There was a silent yet piercingly loud awkwardness in Beth's parents' rejection of my father's inviting conversation attempts. He may not have been discussing the latest current events or the most recent best seller in the *New York Times*, but instead he had kindly baked brownies as an offering of friendship and talked about the weather, as he had done while pumping gas for customers for so many years. Nonetheless, Mr. and Mrs. Smith scorned his gentle simplicity, and as my rage started to boil at the Smiths' snobbishness, and as my embarrassment for my dad heightened, I spilled my milk. While driving home, my father scolded me for my accident by reminding me of the importance of proper manners in the presence of the Smiths. Annoyed by his nagging, I didn't realize that it was the start of my parents' powerful push for me to gain acceptance by this new class of people, triggering my complicated relationship with the upper class that fluctuated between a desire for approval and a refutation of their privileged lifestyle.

As an adolescent, I could no longer laugh at my uncle's annual Christmas Eve jokes. As the adults grew more intoxicated, Uncle Sam inevitably boasted how he was the first in his class to finish the SATs by circling all the A's (he believed it was a race); I, however, quivered despite their amusement. In high school, when I invited my Jewish best friend to celebrate Christmas with us, my holiday spirit turned to dreadful mortification as my relatives cracked racial jokes. How could I explain to Eva, the daughter of two lawyers, who had already traveled

---

1. All names have been changed to protect the identities of people.

to Europe's concentration camps to gain an appreciation for diversity and a tolerance for difference, that my relatives' prejudices were born of low self-esteem? Even at their jobs as gas station attendant and railroad laborer, the men felt that their whiteness entitled them to feel superior to their minority coworkers. Although they may have received meager hourly wages, they clung to their whiteness as an indication of their worthiness. Eva challenged me to enlighten my family, but as a teenager, it was too daunting a task to dispute their cemented thoughts.

I also developed a forceful resistance to my parents' constant pressure to achieve, to run for National Honor Society secretary when I was already overburdened with school responsibilities and a part-time job at the local deli. Furthermore, a self-induced, unreasonable pressure to be the best emerged as an attempt to overcompensate for my class anxieties and the belief that I was not as capable as my peers who had been molded to attend Harvard since they could talk. During high school, I exerted all my mental and physical energy to graduate in the top ten, be elected class president, and earn athletic all-star recognition. On Patriots Day of my senior year, I was awarded the town's prestigious Outstanding Youth Award. Riding in the parade's convertible waving to the people, I should have felt on top of the world. I had succeeded in my goal of paralleling the accomplishments of my peers. Yet I was emotionally exhausted; in my quest to prove my aptitude to my extended community and myself, I had grown engulfed by the fierce spirit of competition.

The pride I felt after winning an academic award or receiving an A had been an unprecedented emotional high that vindicated my self-worth. Yet despite my inner turmoil, studying had always been a haven for me, an undisturbed period in the wee hours of the morning when I would boil water for coffee and type away at the computer (much to my younger brother's dismay, as the clicking of the keyboard would wake him well before the sun). My scholastic endeavors, whether writing a paper or studying for an exam, were solely my own accomplishments, and my intellectual development, despite the countless hours of studying, was a source of great satisfaction and serenity.

My extended family ridiculed my application to Swarthmore (they pronounced it *Sothmoore*); they thought it sounded like a foreign country. Upon my acceptance to Amherst, they again poked fun at the fact that, despite all my hard work, I had only gained acceptance to a state school. But when they learned that Amherst was not the University of Massachusetts and that it was indeed a "smart school," they resented me. My jealous aunt Polly wanted to know why I deserved the opportunity of an elite college education. Likewise, my uncle Jack continuously repeated, "If only you had a clue what it was like to wake up at four o'clock every morning to inspect railroad tracks. Now that's the real world."

Upon entering Amherst, I still hid my anxieties that I was somehow not worthy of acceptance. I could pretend to "walk the walk" and "talk the talk" of my privileged classmates, and, indeed, my peers initially accepted me. However, I carried with me irrational insecurities, trying desperately to fit in despite my raggedy jeans and their designer clothes, their Jeep Cherokees and my bus tickets home, their vacations to Hawaii and my temporary jobs over breaks to make money for the next semester's books. But there was an indefinable moment of personal growth for me during my latter years at Amherst when I quit the lacrosse team (despite its status symbol on campus and its association with all the "popular girls"), when I started eating in the dining halls with classmates with whom I felt comfortable expressing my liberal opinions, and when I began to indulge myself in classes that gave voice to my past and meaning to my identity. I created my own interdisciplinary study about inequality in America stemming from classism and sexism. Culminating my undergraduate experience was the final undertaking of a thesis project on educational inequity.

During my four years at Boston College graduate school, I focused my learning on working-class women's experiences in elite higher education, and it was there that I began to think about social class as a powerful influence on the female self, particularly at top-tier institutions. My graduate school work exposed me to the lack of recognition of working-class culture on college campuses and its negative impact on students from blue-collar backgrounds. In addition to studying critical theory and feminist interpretivism, in graduate school I was enabled to connect personal experiences with theoretical perspectives. I drew upon social reproductive theory as a way to understand my experience of upward mobility in an elite college setting. In writing my doctoral dissertation about the undergraduate experiences of working-class Radcliffe students, I resonated with their experiences of internalized class shame, crossing cultural borders, and being caught between two cultures.

As a professor of higher education, I teach classes on social class equity in higher education and advocate for institutions of higher learning to better support the needs of low-income students. It is validating for me to give conference presentations and to talk with my students in my diversity in higher education class about the need for university administrators to see social class as the third leg in the diversity trinity, next to race and gender. It is personally and professionally satisfying to me that I can take my experience from Amherst College, when I often felt voiceless about being in the minority in terms of my social class background, and now teach future college administrators how to empower new generations of working-class students to have a voice.

Between Scarcity and Plenty

CAMISHA JONES

I was born into a low-income family. My maternal grandmother dropped out of school in the sixth grade to go to work. Both of my grandmothers' work history includes positions cleaning wealthier white people's homes. They took what they had as skills and resources and stretched them to meet the needs of their families. I learned from them how to value and take care of the possessions I have. My mother conceived me when she was seventeen. My parents married the following year, not only because they loved each other but also to give me a good start in the world. My father joined the military in order to provide for our family. I learned from them the value of sacrifice and commitment. Growing up, I often spent the summers with relatives in Lynchburg, Virginia. Usually I would stay with one of my aunts, who like other family members lived in a housing project for a period of time. I would watch my aunt as she cheerfully shared what little she had with others—a loaf of bread to a neighbor, her time with a local Girl Scout troop. She taught me the importance of service and compassion. I took all these lessons with me to college, where I was among predominantly white and wealthier classmates.

I was the first person on my mother's side of the family to go to college. While pursuing my education, I often encountered people who grew up with a different set of class norms. Once while I was in line at a campus eatery, I remember hearing a young lady named

"Muffy" flippantly share how her father had paid off the balance of her credit card and she had just overspent it again. I didn't get my first credit card until my senior year and used it only conservatively; it was in my parents' name, and I didn't want to burden them with unnecessary debt. I recall a college administrator recommending that I ask my parents to take me out to a local seafood restaurant when they came to visit me next. There was no way I was going to ask my parents to take me to some fancy, expensive seafood restaurant while they were still paying for me to attend college. The financial burden of my college education weighed heavily on my mind. I pushed myself to stay focused because I wanted to honor the sacrifice my parents were making to send me to such an expensive university.

I am now someone whose consciousness spans two distinct worlds: a world of financial insufficiency and one of plenty. I know both how to look for values that make the most of my money, as my family has taught me, and I also know how to appreciate unique, upscale experiences valued within wealthier communities. I know how to reuse, repair, and repurpose things to save money, as I was taught growing up, but I am also okay with retiring or replacing objects because they are old, or simply to save time and energy. I am aware of the opportunities and resources readily available within wealthy communities and also intimately aware of the fact that within lower-class communities these opportunities are not as easily accessible, yet there are plenty of doorways to the penal system.

I have learned over the years that each of these worlds often frowns upon the values the other holds. For instance, while in college, I realized that I was in a world where chain restaurants were not considered "quality" dining experiences. I wondered what this said about my family and me? We tend to eat only at chain restaurants. In addition, the movies, plays, books, and television shows we enjoy aren't considered "quality" among wealthier people I interact with. Even now that I have middle-class status, I am uncomfortable when I find myself among much wealthier people who frown upon chain restaurants. I have also experienced the scowls of family members who feel I have been financially wasteful. I recall buying dinner for my father from an upscale grocery store because I wanted to treat him to something special and having him grimace at the price tag. Another time, while I was staying with my grandmother, she accidentally spilled bleach on a pair of my pants. My grandmother took a black magic marker and filled in the small white spot so that the pants would still be wearable. I had already told her I would just throw them out and get a new pair, but I guess that didn't seem to her to be the best course of action.

It's clear to me that among my family members what is most important is finding the best value and saving money. This is seen as "wise," and thus to do differently is seen as foolish. In both worlds, I find myself suppressing some of who I am in order to be accepted. I sit in the midst of different class worlds, and yet I do not entirely fit in either.

I am a family success and expected to "lift as I climb." I am not sure how I got that message, but it's been clear to me since I was a child and dreamt of getting a good job so I could help relatives in their times of need. Perhaps it's because I've watched family members helping each other despite the lack they experience themselves. Perhaps it is because of all the ways my family has encouraged and supported me over the years. Even though I know money alone will not fill the needs, now that I am financially stable, I feel an extreme sense of pressure to give money to relatives whenever I learn that one of them is struggling financially. The needs seem overwhelming. These family members are single parents who hold positions labeled "unskilled labor." They work long hours, weeks without a day off, sometimes more than one job, and still find their lights turned off or their refrigerators empty. When their cars break down or their children act up at school during their work hours, it threatens their job security. From time to time, they are arbitrarily laid off. They usually do not ask for a penny, but whenever I hear of their struggles, I feel a strong sense of obligation to help and to offer advice.

I have a clear understanding of the class experience of my relatives and its impact on me, but it is difficult for me to articulate my own experience of class. Unlike these relatives, my class status allows me to be comfortable and to feel secure. I do not have to worry about having enough money to pay my bills. Even when unexpected expenses arise, I am fortunate enough to have money to cover them. Because of my family background, I am aware that when I make a statement like "I'm broke," it doesn't mean the same as when someone who is impoverished says it. Even when I have periodic anxieties about my money management skills, I am reassured by the fact that I have good credit, credit cards, money in my savings account, and a monthly income that covers my bills with room to spare. Not only that, I have a reliable car, a home that I own, and a career in which my voice and my expertise are usually respected. I rarely take note of these benefits, except for when I am in contact with relatives who struggle financially. Then I realize that my peace of mind is to a large extent a direct benefit of my class status. It is also why I do not often think about how class influences my life. It is a lot easier for me to talk about class from the perspective of my relatives, because to talk about it as someone who is financially stable, I have to admit my comfort is a privilege and that there is a system in place that works more to my benefit than it does for the good of those who are most financially vulnerable.

A Nuyorican's Journey
to Higher Education

Toward Meritocracy or Internalized Classism?

JIM BONILLA

I'm the son of a retired secretary, and I was raised in a single-parent household. In that sense, my story is not so different from that of thousands of working-class New York Puerto Ricans. Straightaway I can tell you Mami would be horrified to hear me refer to us as working class. My mother wholeheartedly bought into the myth that all clean, hardworking Americans were middle class. Even as a "pink-collar" worker, she identified upward with the middle-class (white) people she watched each night on television.

During New York's hot, muggy summers, unlike many of my street friends I got an early opportunity to escape the confines of the city and my working-class background. I was a counselor in a camp for blind children and adults on the Jersey shore. I originally got the job when, as a legally blind camper, I successfully filled in for a counselor who'd gone AWOL after the first week. I was then rehired each summer over the next three years and got to be part of the summer-camp cultural experience. It was not a familiar world for me. The other counselors were from the middle- to upper-middle-class suburbs of New Jersey and Long Island. These counselors were all white, while over half of the campers were kids of color from New York City. Over the course of the summer the counselors became my fast friends, and we'd correspond by mail over the fall and spring. I recall being teased for having an address that had no words in it, only numbers. While my fellow counselors had addresses like Mockingbird

Lane or Maple Court or Jasmine Lane, mine was 111–45 Seventy-Fifth Avenue. They found this endlessly amusing, I suppose in comparison to their suburban experiences, so I didn't take offense. Having risen from the ranks of (working-class) disabled campers, it felt like a privilege to become part of this new fraternity of (middle-class, white, able-bodied) counselors. It would be two of these counselors who would encourage and enable me to attend graduate school thirteen years later.

Other cues at camp served to remind me that mine was a "different" reality. Most of the counselors at camp attended private universities or colleges. I was puzzled by the rationale for the staggering expense of a private-college education. However, it was obvious that my fellow counselors were impressed and often awed by counselors who made it into the private elite colleges with names like Swarthmore or Bowdoin or the University of Chicago. I wondered to myself what was so special about these places that merited the hushed comments like, "He goes to Swarthmore, he must be really smart (or really rich)." In my second season at camp I was accepted to the State University of New York College at Cortland, the first one from my family this side of the Caribbean to attend an institution of higher education. Given no one else on my block was college bound, at the time I thought my acceptance to state college was a big deal. I quickly surmised that it was not on par with making it into the "privates" like my co-counselors. This was my first introduction to the class pecking order that is higher education in America.

After college I worked first as a disability activist and then as a community organizer in poor white and black communities. In addition to my early work as a community organizer, later I co-designed courses on classism in graduate school. Because of these experiences, I was under the impression then that I had class issues down. However, the sense of being a stranger in a strange land would come back to nag me again once I completed my doctorate at the University of Massachusetts at Amherst and began my career as an academic. Although UMass was the flagship campus of a great state university system, it was my faculty colleagues with doctorates from places like Yale, Princeton, or Harvard who elicited the same hushed tones of reverence from other faculty that I first heard during my camp days. I discovered that many of my new colleagues grew up being read to at a very early age. They spoke of childhood homes that had bookshelves and whole libraries devoted to great works of literature. If their parents were not themselves faculty, many were the offspring and siblings of college graduates. In a home where the first language wasn't English, growing up I can't recall ever having seen a book in my house.

I came to embrace reading as a child thanks to my love of Marvel Comics, which I diligently purchased weekly with my fifty-cent chores allowance. A secretary friend of my mother had a son who worked for Doubleday publishers in Manhattan. Her son was fifteen years my senior and arranged to get me the entire Hardy Boys series for my tenth birthday. I was stunned beyond all measure. Now I had my own library with hard-backed books, complete with jacket covers! Sadly this thrill was not something I could share with my street amigos. At minimum it would have elicited some strange stares and, more likely, choice name-calling ("egghead" being one polite version). So my collection became my secret stash. It was not until I arrived at the hallowed halls of the ivory tower as a first-year assistant professor that I finally realized how common books and even libraries were in the homes of my middle- to owning-class colleagues.

It has been nearly two decades since I completed my doctorate and joined the faculty of a small private university in the Midwest. I've come to love this life of the academic for its attention to reason, justice, and equity, as well as the independence and job security it affords me. This seeming meritocratic utopia is a far cry from my childhood experiences of emotional and occasional physical violence, racism, and dependence on authority.

As a faculty member I conducted lots of research into issues of racism in the academy. Since 1986, I've taught courses on racism using my experience as a person of color to ground my teaching, research, and service to the Latino community and others. As Douglas Brent observed, "Middle-class folks expect rewarding careers. Other folks have jobs. And if they are lucky, the jobs aren't too bad. Compared with the rest of my family, I'm lucky."[1] Yet for me the academic life also brings ambivalence. This struck home for me at a recent all-campus meeting called to discuss the implications of the economic downturn

---

1. Brent, D. (1996). "Outsiders." In J. Ryan and C. Sackrey, *Strangers in Paradise: Academics from the Working Class.* New York, NY: University Press of America, Inc., p. 267

to our university. Rather than lay off staff, our president had chosen instead to temporarily institute reductions of 2.5 percent to retirement matches. Two faculty got up to chide the president and the trustees about the lack of faculty input into this decision. Then one of our young, working-class coaches rose and spoke with emotion, "We here in higher ed live in a bubble. In the real world people are losing their jobs all over the country. My wife just got laid off from Target. I'm lucky and grateful to just have a job. If faculty don't like it here they should leave and try getting a job out in the real world." Part of me was initially outraged that this young, nonfaculty person would dare speak to my colleagues in such an uncivil manner. But part of me knew he was partially right. Some faculty were simply put out that our neat, orderly, professional middle-class world should be disturbed by anything so pedestrian as the worst economic downturn since the Great Depression. My ambivalence is this: part of me is drawn to the "bubble" that is life in the academy. Higher education has become my gateway into the middle class. But I also realize that there are times where I collude by maintaining status barriers that reproduce the micro-inequities that reflect a larger class system. Not unlike me in my summer camp days, when I was the only working-class counselor of color on staff, I do want to be a part of "a community of scholars." I've organized faculty book groups to foster community, but they've excluded staff on the grounds that faculty issues are different from those of staff.

My internalized classism can be triggered by the fear that my writing or research will be criticized as "not scholarly enough." The ever-present dread that someday I'll be found out and judged as an impostor in the court of higher education is just below the surface. Even after twenty-plus years in the ivory tower, the sense that someday I'll be found out and judged as not worthy lingers. At the same time part of me wants to believe the academy represents for me a meritocracy where status is earned by excellence in teaching, research, and service, not simply conferred based on unearned privilege, connections, or financial advantage. (Otherwise how to reconcile the value of a Harvard degree vs. one from a state college?) Yet even in the midst of this seeming meritocracy there exist many undercurrents of classism.

I confess to being occasionally irked by white, mostly working-class staff who complain that faculty are pompous, out-of-touch elites. They have the temerity to question why faculty merit being treated like high priests simply because we have doctorates, while staff are treated as second-class citizens. I once tried explaining (rather defensively, I might add) that faculty status and perks are based on actual merit, not just as teachers (after all, many staff teach), but as scholars who also give service to their disciplines and to their communities on and off campus. It's not unlike the elitism of the NBA, I rationalized, where elite athletes are given better salaries and higher status based on the merits of their performance. With a higher education, the myth goes, you must prove yourself by the brilliance of your teaching, research, and service. What could be more equitable? Yet it is painful to hear staff speak of feeling disrespected and not getting the kinds of professional development opportunities faculty receive; after all, my mother could have been one of those staff people. Once, after I had gleefully announced that a paper I wrote had been accepted for presentation at an international conference in Latvia, one staff member coolly remarked, "It must be nice."

Then one day last fall, a first-year undergraduate unintentionally poked an even larger hole in my wall of rationalization. We had attended a campus seminar on classism where class privilege in American higher education was discussed. Early in the day, a facilitator had led us in a seemingly innocuous activity called "Common Ground." This consisted of a series of questions aimed at about one hundred faculty, staff, and students, who were supposed to stand if their answers were yes. For example, one question was, "Were you raised by a single parent?" I stood. Another question was, "Are you the first to have gone to college from your family?" I stood. Separately, faculty were then asked to stand if they were raised in a working-class community. Again I stood, and this time I was the only person standing in the room. I took my seat afterward thinking little about the activity. I knew my roots, and it came as little surprise that most of my colleagues were either owning or middle class.

Later that week while grabbing a quick dinner in the student dining hall (before my night class), I was approached by an unfamiliar new student. White, blond, and dressed similarly to her peers, she came up to me and said, "Professor Bonilla, thank you so much for doing what you did in the workshop on class. It was very brave." I didn't recall having done anything brave, so I asked, "What did I do exactly?" It was at this point in the conversation that she got very quiet and whispered, 'Until you stood up, I had never met a professor who was working class like me. I've felt completely alone here until I saw you standing up."

For someone who is trained to seek out new ideas, I really hate it when my well-constructed paradigms tumble with so little effort. What this first-year student from the working class had just done was point out just how unwelcoming a place private higher education still is for young people raised other than middle or upper class. Her words made it clearer to me that in my efforts to foreground institutional racism in the academy, I had put issues of class far into the background. While I can be eloquent on how higher education continues to exclude folks of color, I rarely focused on how the academy (and my role in it) mirrors America's larger class divide. In less than two minutes, this young, white, working-class woman had uncomfortably reminded me that many of the same invisible barriers that confront students of color in the ivory tower also persist for today's white, low-income, and working-class students. This was an "aha" moment because I thought I'd already negotiated this minefield. I thought I had "gotten" class, but I forgot that unlike racism, classism in the academy is often invisible, but just as pervasive. Whereas race is generally more obvious, with class identities you never know.

The title of this piece began with a reference to a journey in higher education—toward meritocracy or internalized classism? I can offer no simple answers. What little I can offer is thanks to a first-year, white working-class student and the "taking stock" she provoked. Perhaps the answer to the question of whether mine is a story of meritocracy or internalized classism is "neither and both." Until students like this first-year young woman can enter the academy without having to fear that they don't belong, or feel they have to "pass" as middle class, we really haven't made it to the land of meritocracy. Until she and more like her can easily recognize faculty who reflect this part of her identity, her class story, the myth of meritocracy breathes on. I see now that we often can't know the effects of disclosing our identities to others. Who knows how many other working-class students could feel some relief at hearing their professors tell their class stories? Like my camp counselor friends did for me, I can play a role in encouraging poor and working-class students to avail themselves of higher education's promise. I can also be an advocate for greater affordability and accessibility for lower-income students of all colors. As long as we keep standing up, internalized classism cannot claim a total victory.

My Parents' Hands Are
on My Back

CHRISTINE OVERALL

I grew up in a Toronto suburb of tiny bungalows. Although we did not go hungry, my father, a chronic alcoholic and World War II veteran, was sometimes unemployed. I often wore secondhand clothes, or clothes that I made or others made for me. We lived on my mother's careful budgeting, and it allowed no luxuries.

A common stereotype about working-class people is that, unlike middle-class people, they do not value higher education. And there is some truth to the stereotype. Working-class people know they need to take care of themselves: education should be practical and pragmatic; it should be aimed toward getting a job and making a steady income. From that perspective, education for its own sake is almost incomprehensible; at best it's an effete indulgence for folks with more money than they know what to do with: don't waste time staying in school; you don't need to read a lot of books to know how the world works.

Of course, the reality is that working-class families often cannot afford to send their kids to college or university. So the issue of postsecondary education is irrelevant. And if nobody goes, then nobody knows what it's like. If you've never met anyone who benefited from college or university, it's easy to dismiss higher education. If you've never felt a need or a longing to study, you don't understand why it might be rewarding.

My family was different. They valued university so highly, they could recognize and accept no other alternative for their children. Education was, in their minds, without a doubt the way up and out—indeed, the only way to escape.

My mother came from a relatively wealthy background. She was the daughter of a self-made man who had only an eighth-grade education but worked his way up to senior management in his firm. Hence, my mother's family came through the Depression without suffering in the way that other families did. My mother's family not only had all the food they needed; they even employed a maid and rented vacation homes in the summer.

After finishing high school at a young age, my mother longed to go to university herself, but her parents saw no point in it. After all, her father was a successful man, and with very little education. My mother lacked the independence, both financial and personal, to make her own way.

When my mother married, she chose a man "beneath" her, in class terms. My father came from a working-class background. His father was never entirely out of work during the Depression, but his employer, Bell Telephone, put him on part-time work so that it could avoid firing him and other employees. Thus, my father's parents raised their children on an income derived from only two or three days' work each week. My father finished high school and almost immediately joined the Canadian military in order to do his part in World War II. To my knowledge he never aspired to further education, although his postwar employment history often demonstrated the gaps in his knowledge.

As a result of their disparate backgrounds—one longing for the education she could not have, the other missing the education he needed—my parents pushed me, and my younger brothers, to have intellectual ambitions. The main symbol for those ambitions was reading books. Every week the whole family visited the library. My parents loved to read and regarded it as normal for children to spend hours alone with a book. I was also expected to excel in school. Top marks were just expected; I was never rewarded for them. Other children would receive small treats for a good report card, but in my life, marks of A+ were supposed to be the norm. I came to fear some nameless, unexpressed disaster if I was not the best student in all my classes.

Throughout my childhood I was told I would someday go to university. I believed there was no alternative, and that I would be a failure if I did not enroll. Nonetheless, my parents were not willing to provide me with much financial support after high school. Perhaps they were not able to, although they found some money to fund part of my younger brothers' university costs. I was allowed to continue to live at home while attending a downtown university, but it was made clear I would have to pay for my tuition fees, books, and supplies—not to mention the expenses of the one-hour-each-way commute to classes, and whatever clothes I thought necessary for being a student.

Fortunately for me, I won a four-year scholarship that paid for my tuition, with some money left over for books. I financed my other needs by working full time during the summer and part time during the school year. But I lived in terror that I would lose my scholarship. Having come to believe that all that mattered about me was my capacity to get good grades, anything below an A average each year would mean not only that my scholarship would be withdrawn, but also that I was not a smart person, that all my parents' dreams for me would be shattered, and that I would have no future. I felt as if I had my parents' hands on my back, pushing me relentlessly out of their world and into the world of higher education. University was terra incognita; there was no family road map that I could consult. Yet falling back into their world was unthinkable. I would either be pushed out of it, or I would simply fall face forward in defeat.

I succeeded. Many years later I am a tenured professor at one of Canada's strongest universities. Yet I still feel my parents' hands in the middle of my back, pushing me. Almost every time I give a public lecture, lead a workshop, or I teach a class, I'm afraid of failure. Failure will mean not only humiliation, but the revelation that I do not belong in the class I worked so hard to enter. I was pushed out of my working-class origins, but I continue to fear, however irrationally, that the academic world might push me back.

PART III

Middle Class

THE CONTRIBUTORS IN THIS PART GREW UP IN fairly diverse backgrounds, lending support to the fact that the term "middle class" is a very loose and elastic concept. As one author put it, "My family and I existed as so many others did and still do: in the strange and shifting ether of the middle class."

Some came from consciously "upper middle class" families, while others grew up in secure, but materially less well off, circumstances. A few contributors focus on the "cultural" and "social" capital their class status provided them, while others, people of color, point out the complexities and difficulties that race and racism forced them to confront. Many discuss their awareness of their own "class privilege," and several white contributors note their "white skin privilege" as well.

By definition, of course, being in the middle means that you stand in between, with some above and some below you. As the contributors recall their early years, they remind us of how open and idealistic children are—"that kids are much more adept than adults at bridging divides." One author, Pamela Burrows, remembers the moment that a girl named Marie became her best friend, and the good times they had over the next eight years. They stayed friends even though Pam knew at some level that her mother disapproved of the relationship. "I suspect that it had something to do with Marie's mom having bleached platinum-blond hair," Burrows writes, "and with her South Philly accent, with the fact that her dad didn't wear a suit to work, the fact that some of his work wasn't necessarily legal."

It takes awhile for critical life experiences to teach children the reality of American life and class, that there are people and groups "above" and "below." For author Monica Crumback, that moment came one wintry day when she entered her elementary school friend's house, on what seemed like a homogeneous, solidly middle-class street, and surprised her friend's mom, who sat at the bottom of the steps going up to the second floor. The house was very cold, and she looked "like she was freezing . . . a blanket wrapped snuggly around her shoulders and . . . a cup of something hot in her hands." The child "was embarrassed and felt strange because I had never had to find the one warm place in my whole big house and then curl my young self around it as greedily as I had just seen a grown woman do." The experience of being in the middle continues into adulthood and can vary as one's own status shifts depending on various circumstances.

In a society where racism remains a fact of life, race and class often become confounded, and the privileges that a middle-class status may bring are lessened for African Americans. The Reverend John Vaughn grew up in a well-respected, professional middle-class family, but tells us that "at an early age, I was introduced to the idea that an 'Oreo cookie' was sometimes more than just a sweet treat." Vaughn had to deal with the taunts and teasing of his black peers, but he also had to endure the condescension of whites, who wanted to remind him that he wasn't like the others—that is, he was a good one. In discussing and examining his continued life experiences, Vaughn emphasizes the diversity of black American experiences, along with the diversity of white America. Just as there is no one "white community," neither does there exist a single "black community." And class remains one dominant factor that divides both communities, along with our understanding of both.

"Better Be Street"

My Adventures in Cross-Class Romance

POLLY TROUT

The first time I thought about class I was thirteen. I met a stoner boy in a heavy metal T-shirt at the bus stop in Tacoma, and we got to talking. I missed my bus, he missed his bus, then we started making out on the bench. He pulled up and said, "Hey, so what does your father do?"

"He's a lawyer," I said.

"That's funny." He frowned lopsided, eyes glancing down to the left. "You sure don't act like a rich girl."

He never called.

My father was a corporate attorney, a deacon in our evangelical church, and a sociopath. You know the opening scene in *Blue Velvet* with the suburban house and picket fence that looks tidily bourgeois on the outside but is seething with subterranean evil? That pretty much sums up my childhood. I learned early on that money doesn't buy love or safety, plus never trust a man in a suit. I credit my father for my lifelong fetish for the outlaw with a heart of gold.

At seventeen I fled the suburbs for a hippie liberal arts college in the woods and immersed myself in the counterculture along with all the other liberal white middle-class misfits and freaks. We played at being poor while ignoring the safety net of privilege that invisibly floated under our insular self-absorption. We were knowledge class, and our social status derived from our cultural capital, not our income. Wild and wounded, I obsessed on an endless string of boys from my new tribe: the self-styled working-class poet who wrote songs about growing up in a small town and working in a slaughterhouse, even though both his parents were white-collar professionals. The artist who lived in the cockroach-infested boardinghouse pretending to be like the Beat Generation writer Charlie Bukowski and spending his trust-fund checks on heroin. Life revolved around books, torrid sexual affairs, and partying. Academia was the perfect place to escape from reality, which I excelled at, so I went on to graduate school, eventually getting a PhD in the academic study of religion from Boston University.

I probably would have stayed cocooned in that insular ivory bubble if it wasn't for my erotic fetish for bad boys on the margins. The other day I asked my sister, "Why are working-class men so much sexier than middle-class men?"

She took a drag off her cigarette and thought about it. "I don't know. Especially blue-collar men who read. Nothing's sexier than that."

"Bell hooks would know," I replied. "There should be a bell hooks hotline for questions like these."

"Contemporary focus on victimization rarely acknowledges that the erotic is a space of transgression that can undermine the politics of domination," writes hooks, in her essay "Good Sex." The American mainstream often assumes that nontraditional sexual relationships are sites of exploitation, rather than sites of equality and mutual transformation. What saved me from stalling out in a shallow form of sexual tourism was my spiritual practice. I believe that there is a spiritual dimension to reality that infuses and connects all living beings. I believe that we are all a single human family, and that each person is of equal and infinite worth, a unique and evolving art project. Culture and class and gender divide us, but our spiritual and biological lives draw us together. I believe that the life of spirit calls us to live fearlessly, authentically, compassionately. I believe in the healing and transformative power of love. Also, that nothing dissolves artificial boundaries more quickly than a really good crush. I could have made it through grad school and taught indefinitely without understanding a damn thing about class. I discovered the blind spots where my white privilege lurked through endless all-night conversations with people I loved enough to listen to deeply, drunk and naked, inspired and openhearted.

The radicalization of my class consciousness was a long, slow, painful process that took years and a series of heartbreaks. In Boston I dated an Irish Italian construction worker from a blue-collar family who was moonlighting as a middle-management drug trafficker for extra cash. We got along great when we were alone, but the relationship burned out when we realized that we hated each other's friends. Mike's idea of a the perfect Sunday afternoon was to go to a backyard barbecue at a friend's house, where all the men would watch football in the living room while all the women gossiped in the kitchen. I preferred endless philosophical conversations with my grad school cronies. My world bored him, and his world bored me.

Possessed by a classic case of baby fever in my early thirties, I reverted to the mating rituals of my tribe of "Cultural Creatives" and married a good friend who came from a white middle-class background and had inherited a cushy trust fund. Class warfare destroyed our marriage. Although we started the relationship politically compatible, once our daughters were born, an invisible philosophical fault line gaped into a canyon, and we stopped making sense to each other. Formerly free-spirited and idealistic, he seemed to become a conservative overnight under the influence of fatherhood. He looked at the kids and thought, "I've got to get my shit together because these tiny fragile beings depend utterly on me. That means that I need to become careful, cautious, and put the family first." I looked at the kids and thought, "I've got to get my shit together because it is my job to turn these tiny primates into strong and ethical women—this means that I need to stop being so narcissistic and set a good example for them, fearlessly living my values and helping create the kind of world I can be proud to leave them in." Neither of us was wrong.

My commitment to being a good mom led to a renewed commitment to social justice work. I started seeing the world through the eyes of the people I worked with, who came from economically marginalized communities. I learned that the most important part of culturally competent social justice work is the ability to be both humble about my own ignorance and genuinely willing to learn and change. My skills as a critical thinker and gonzo anthropologist came in handy. I learned how to treat everybody like a human being, which means I approach each new person with respect, compassion, and reluctance to judge. I learned how to be an effective and valued ally, and as my skill set grew I realized that more and more of my close women friends came from the working class and marginalized communities.

By the time the divorce rolled around, my patience with middle-class complacency was at an all-time low. I was nearing forty. Most of my yuppie friends had sold out and were someplace between comfortably numb and passively miserable. Then I fell madly, passionately, unrequitedly in love with a street warrior who ran the local needle exchange, who did me the enormous favor of relentlessly deconstructing my unexamined class privilege over the course of three excruciating years. I no longer identified with or conformed to middle-class cultural expectations, but I also saw that I would never be part of any other class. I became a social anomaly, a spiritual experiment in undoing classism. Once when I was tutoring a homeless teen for the GED, she eloquently broke down the elaborate social hierarchy of the streets for me, with squatters at the top and posers at the bottom. I asked her, what would you call someone who had a safe place to live but was as real as a squatter, who never faked it?

She thought about it for a while. "I guess I'd call them a human being," she said. Street people taught me how to be a human being.

My current boyfriend is a half Mexican gutter-punk welder from the ghetto. He is glorious. We like each other's friends, or most of the important ones anyway. His world fascinates me, and my world fascinates him. We stay up all night talking, drunk and naked, inspired and openhearted. I am still part of the knowledge class; I'm not a poser, and don't try to pass myself off as street. I'm just myself, everywhere and with everybody. As my spiritual practice deepens, it becomes progressively easier to let go of status and social norms altogether, focusing all my energy on being loving and real with as little baggage as possible. In places where I used to take structures of domination for granted, there is an empty space of freedom and potential that fills me with joy.

Next, I'm going to work on deconstructing my lingering class prejudice against rich people. Men in suits still creep me out. But you know, they're human beings too. Just not all that hot.

> Scorn your mind
> Just feel the pain
> It's what makes us human
> It keeps us all the same
>
> —The Gits, "Cut My Skin It Makes Me Human"

It's Who You Know and How You Talk

BETSY LEONDAR-WRIGHT

I consider myself extremely lucky to have had several staff jobs at nonprofit organizations whose missions I believed in. After my twenties, I never again had to get a "day job," but was able to get paychecks for full-time work on the cause dearest to my heart, economic justice in the United States.

But was it luck that got me those jobs? Or did it have something to do with my upper-middle-class background? I'm guessing it was my background.

How do nonprofits decide whom to hire? Virtually all of them have affirmative-action policies for race. Gender diversity usually takes care of itself, as the majority of nonprofit employees are women; and at least in Massachusetts since the 1990s, GLBT acceptance is mostly a given. But class-based affirmative action is almost unheard of. I suspect there's widespread bias in favor of hiring people from more-privileged class backgrounds.

It's not that any hiring committees were impressed that I went to elite schools, Exeter for my last year of high school and then Princeton for three years. On the contrary: I used to hide the P-word, after discovering that it was a conversation stopper in certain liberal and progressive circles. The fact that I had dropped out of Princeton and gotten my BA from the non–Ivy League but still academically sound Boston College was very handy for making my résumé more typical, without any eye-catching elite status.

No, the ways that my class background helped me get hired were more subtle than blatant educational bias. My experience illustrates the ways that "social capital" (who you know) and "cultural capital" (the knowledge and style valued by those in power) operate in the nonprofit sector.

First, by the time I applied for my first staff job, I already had a résumé full of involvements related to the organization's program work, all done as a volunteer. The financial security of my family of origin had conditioned me to be cavalier about money, and I worked only part time in my twenties, sharing rent and wearing secondhand clothes, so that I could spend most of my time as an unpaid volunteer. I entered my thirties with only $500 in savings, but that low-budget lifestyle, which hadn't seemed self-interested to me at the time, turned out to be a good investment, because my volunteer work helped me get desirable jobs with salary and benefits later.

Second, I had a lot of social contacts with people in a position to hire. Many of my personal friends and fellow volunteers from my twenties ended up in management positions at nonprofits.

Usually I didn't actually know anyone on the hiring committee, but often I knew people who knew them, or people they respected.

Once I applied for a job focused on a certain issue that I had never worked on before. How to impress them? I called up my friend who was a small-magazine editor and offered to do a book review about that very issue; it came out in print before my first interview, so I was able to hand the interviewer a published article closely related to the organization's work. I didn't get that job, but I did get a second interview. Similar friends-of-friends informal references helped me get the jobs I did get. It was easy to find out on the grapevine what an organization's visions and problems were. I got one job by stressing my fund-raising experience, after I'd asked around among my acquaintances and found out that the organization was in financial trouble, a fact they weren't yet revealing publicly.

Third, I spoke the lingo. In interviews, I talked about advocacy to the advocates, feminism to the feminists, leadership development to the community organizers, and organizational development to the nonprofit managers. This wasn't a calculated move on my part; I felt comfortable with the interviewers, and we shared some frames of reference, learned in college or in majority-professional-middle-class civic groups.

Once a majority-white hiring committee offered me a job as an organizer in a community of color, choosing me over some candidates of color, because they said they liked how I talked about antiracism and diversity. I turned the job down and told them if they really wanted outreach to people of color, they should hire a person of color. What possessed them to think my diversity talk would make me better at the job than other people's life experience?

Was I the best candidate for all the jobs I got, or were there other well-qualified people who might have added class diversity to the organizations, but who knew less of the lingo and had fewer social contacts? There's no way to know, but my guess is that I fit the profile of who tends to get hired for program jobs at nonprofits, publishers, and foundations.

I've been part of many hiring committees in which we intended to look only at qualifications relevant to the actual job, but in fact we were wowed by résumés full of internships at organizations we respected, political buzzwords, and references from leaders we admired. Talking about "empowerment" would trump actually having been empowered through grassroots participation in community organizing. We would never have *consciously* looked down on an applicant who went to a public or community college. But the lack of internships and volunteer jobs made many public college students' résumés look thinner than those from elite private colleges, which often provide stipends for internships, and where many students can afford to take unpaid internships. We didn't intentionally discriminate against people whose references were from the private sector, such as 7-Eleven managers, but our eyes were caught by the references from nonprofits that shared our values, sometimes from particular people that we knew. We liked people who talked about the books that had raised their awareness of our cause, and sometimes we overlooked those who had learned from struggling with their own class oppression. The right way to talk about race is one of the litmus tests for progressive hiring, but sometimes changes in the right lingo sweep across college campuses and professional conferences without most working-class and poor people being informed. A shallow gloss of political correctness sometimes trumped a deeper understanding expressed through personal stories and self-taught ideas.

These class biases are probably even more blatant in other kinds of not-for-profit organizations than in the type of nonprofit I've worked for, the small progressive ones. Steve Early, author of *Civil Wars in U.S. Labor*, has documented a trend among the new service worker unions of hiring college-educated organizers and managers, breaking the labor tradition of hiring rank-and-file workers. And most big nonprofit agencies put educational requirements, such as a BA or MA, in their job notices.

The truth is that many nonprofits are desperately in need of the social connections and the cultural strengths that working-class and poor people could bring them, but they don't identify that need and don't have any effective way of evaluating candidates for it during the hiring process. To be successful, mission-driven nonprofits need to persuade and recruit people from diverse communities, most of which are working class, impoverished, or lower middle class; therefore contacts in those communities, and ability to talk the way they talk and operate by local norms, should make a candidate a hot prospect. But that's rarely the case, except in terms of ethnically specific outreach. Many groups put "bilingual/bicultural" in their job descriptions, but who asks for class-bilingual or class-bicultural?

Many efforts to hire people of color end up considering only those with professional parents. The "diverse pool" without which many an affirmative action hire doesn't move forward is often filled with international people who came to the United States for graduate school, Asian Americans with professional parents, and other relatively class-privileged people of color. For example, for a public health outreach position in a low-income Dominican neighborhood, someone who came from Argentina to get a PhD might be hired instead of a Dominican high school graduate from the neighborhood. The silence about class is hushing up what a terrible job the nonprofit sector is doing on hiring people of color who have come from poverty, as well as working-class and poor whites. Racial diversity is important for its own sake, but it can't serve as a stand-in for class diversity or it ends up helping primarily elites of color.

Ironically, low pay and long hours tilt hiring pools toward women from privileged class backgrounds. Most social service agencies, publishers, and arts organizations, chronically financially strapped, pay one-quarter to two-thirds the amount that the same skills would earn in the government or private business sectors. And some famous community-organizing groups have been known to openly violate minimum wage and overtime pay laws, historically requiring seventy-hour weeks for subsistence pay. There's a long tradition of elite women volunteering for charitable causes, as Susan Ostrander's book *Women of the Upper Class* describes. This tradition continues, as women from professional families work for nonprofit organizations for a fraction of what they could earn elsewhere. If you have a husband or partner with a lucrative career, or an inheritance in your future, you can live comfortably while only earning a small nonprofit salary. It's not uncommon for an applicant pool to include only graduates of private colleges. Community organizing and social-service jobs often get no applicants who actually grew up in the low-income neighborhood where the work would be done or the services provided. First-generation college students, many with heavy debt and low-income family members to support, often look for the best-paying job they can get, avoiding the unstable jobs at small nonprofits if they can.

Small nonprofits that depend on donations and foundation grants also can't afford to do much formal staff training or on-the-job development for promotions. Instead they rely on people who show up ready to roll, with high-level skills acquired elsewhere. "Management" is a dirty word in some liberal and progressive circles, but in fact all nonprofits need good financial management, program management, and personnel management. Instead of making management skills explicit and making a plan either to hire for them or develop them, nonprofits sometimes hire people who have acquired a more-or-less managerial outlook from their class backgrounds—or else they may hire people without enough experience to effectively do unwritten parts of the job description. Neither approach serves them well. Turnover is very high at most small nonprofits. If a study were done of those who leave, especially from higher-level positions, I suspect they would tend to come from lower class backgrounds than those who stay.

The most intentionally anti-classist organizations I've been part of, United for a Fair Economy (UFE) and Class Action, both have policies against putting formal education requirements in job notices. If writing and editing skills are needed, the job notice should just say that, and it shouldn't matter whether the skills were gained at college, were learned on the job, or were self-taught. Both have a maximum pay ratio of two to one and relatively high entry-level wages. Class Action includes class in its affirmative action policy. But these policies are unusual, and they aren't enough to eliminate classism in hiring. One year when UFE decided to prioritize giving internships to public and community college students and so publicized its internship program heavily at those colleges, the number of applicants from public colleges was exactly zero.

It's hard to imagine how hiring could become completely non-class-biased in the current political and economic system. Especially since the Great Recession of 2008 to 2010, many small nonprofits are very financially fragile. When folding is a realistic fear, spending scarce time and money on slower, more thoughtful hires or internal staff development is difficult. Understaffed and overstressed organizations can't handle too much cultural difference among the staff, and class diversity adds more layers of cultural difference.

But to change the political and economic system, this is something we *have* to change. We're not going to create a fairer society if our organizations are so class biased that they have a shortage of working-class cultural strengths and are deprived of the insights of those who are living with the problems firsthand. It's time to practice what we preach.

Childhood Friendship

When Class Didn't Matter

PAMELA BURROWS

In first grade my best friend asked me what my report card marks were in grammar. I didn't know the word "grammar," so she had to explain a little bit. Turned out mine were "excellent," while hers were "needs improvement" or something of the sort. I had, at that tender young age, spent less than a moment considering how to frame my sentences, or what word fit best where. Like her, I spoke pretty much like my parents spoke, and the result was that I was perceived as a smart, well-spoken child, and she was perceived, well, pretty much as a kid from South Philly.

Marie was my best friend from the moment we met. We weren't that similar in some ways, but we were instantly close. We would be so for about the next eight years, even though for the last four we lived in different states. We established our habit of spending hours of every night on the phone early on, when I was still so shy I begged my mother every night to call Marie's mom first, and then put us on the phone. I never quite understood my mother's look of distaste when I requested this. I don't think it really had to do with the shame of having a child paralyzed by shyness. It was more like the look of horror when I suggested to my mother that she and Marie's mother should be best friends too, so the four of us could hang out, or at least they could enjoy coffee and conversation while we were spinning our fantasy worlds. My mom was never as taken as I was with the simple beauty of such an arrangement.

Now I suspect that it had something to do with Marie's mom having bleached platinum-blond hair, and with her South Philly accent, with the fact that her dad didn't wear a suit to work, the fact that some of his work wasn't necessarily legal.

Marie stayed with my family quite a bit during our friendship. We went to the same school, so she could borrow my uniforms and be good to go. I still don't know the details of what was going on with her family. At the time I just thought my mother was remarkably accommodating about endless sleepovers. When her mom did come to pick her up, we would hide one of her shoes and pretend to be unable to find it, thus buying a little more time together, though pretending to look for a shoe wasn't exactly the most fun we'd ever had.

Marie stood up when we saw the film *Rocky* and said, "That's my neighborhood! That's my neighborhood!" I was in awe of her bravery, her nonchalance at being noticed, as well as her growing up near Rocky! My mother was mortified and told the story for years. It was cute, but clearly embarrassing.

When Marie first saw my house her eyes got really big and she said, "You live in a *mansion!*" When I first saw hers I was taken aback that some kids lived in apartments; I had somehow thought those were reserved for bohemian young adults, but never families.

Marie introduced me to playing at open fire hydrants, neighborhoods with corners where people "hung out" and some corners that were safer to walk by than others, the endearment "honey-child," heavenly sugared fried dough bits at the Italian market. My family took her out to plays. We loved to tell people we were sisters, with ten siblings at home. Once a lady we were renting a house from, "down the shore," asked my mom how she managed with all those children, causing great confusion, as she had only me.

We grew up. We drifted apart. The turning point for me was when she invited me to go make out with boys under the boardwalk—another cultural experience that wasn't available to me in other parts of my life. But I was skittish, and not nearly as curious as you'd think. We suddenly had less and less to talk about.

I've been back in touch with her as an adult. She's done well, with a successful career, a few beautiful children, and a loving husband. I still don't know if I could find my way around her world without her help, but likely for different reasons these days.

Did I learn anything from this? Why even bring it up? Maybe all I've learned is that kids are much more adept than adults at bridging divides. I knew as a child that we were less similar than we might have been, in so many ways that the world around us deemed important, ways that meant our mothers would have probably avoided interaction as much as possible were it not for us. We didn't name that divide and then try to bridge it; we just were who we were, and the differences in grammar and recreational choices meant no more than the differences in our heights or hair color. I miss those days sometimes.

Finding Myself in the Middle

MONICA CRUMBACK

When I was a very young child, I knew that I was rich. And, considering my family's in-ground pool and my own ongoing private education, you would have had a tough pull convincing me otherwise. The "oohs" and the "aahs" that escaped my friends' mouths at the sight of my pool rang too loudly and pleasantly in my ears; and I was equally pleased that my mother chauffeured me off to school every morning while all my friends, poor things, took the rickety old bus to the public elementary.

So even though I could clearly remember my schoolteacher father recruiting friends and relatives to help dig out our pool and stretch the liner, and even though my private school was a two-room parochial shack of uneven quality, I knew that I was rich. Such was the certainty of my very young life.

When I was a slightly older child, however, I began to suspect that my family might be merely upper class—and that only marginally. In fact, by the fifth grade, when private school gave way to public, I began to fret over my status. You could almost have called it a slowly encroaching panic, really, when I started to see kids wearing jewelry—*gold* jewelry. And these same kids wore lovely clothes, sporting different and impressive outfits for every day of the week. They carried backpacks with designer labels, while I had no such finery. I had yard-sale clothes and hand-me-downs. I also had to rethink—right from scratch—what my class stature actually was. But at least I didn't have to do it alone.

It was the mom of one of my friends who first helped me to find and worry about a specific flaw in my upper-class self-definition. It was the result of something that she said, actually, even though she meant it as a compliment. "Monica always looks so nice," she told her daughter, admonishing my friend for not tucking in her shirt. I stood there, over-hearing and instantly horrified. Because I knew for a fact that rich kids did not look *nice*. No, they looked cool as they annoyed their indulgent parents with their ever-changing styles complemented by garish and expensive belts and purses, difficult hairdos, dangling earrings, and bright pink bangle bracelets—none of which I had.

So, as it turned out, rich kids were enviable, well-accessorized rogues of a sort—and I was obviously not among them. Instead, I was just a plain if nice-looking kid with a tucked-in shirt and a home-dug pool. It seems silly now, but the shame back then was immediate, huge, and heavy. Or at least it felt that way, until it got a lot colder.

That winter was awful. If I remember correctly, though, I didn't care on one day in particular. My quest was too urgent: I was headed to my friend's house to flaunt my brand-new Christmas leg warmers. They were pink, I think, unless I was wearing both the pink *and* the white pair over my well-worn corduroy pants. Either way, I was a walk-ing fluorescent fashion disaster. But my ego was none the wiser, and I was itchy-keen to show off. So I set out on the quick sidewalk jaunt feeling proud of myself, shaking hard from the cold and thanking God that I had so little distance to go.

My friend lived just two doors down from me in a house that resem-bled my own: old and drafty and featuring steep staircases that were paired with questionable railings. Sure, my house was probably more kempt than hers, but that distinction existed because of my mother's meticulous housekeeping. Otherwise, the entire neighborhood was much the same—not a vinyl window or a speck of lead-free paint in sight. But, because we were a neighborhood in the old-style sense of the word, we were allowed the bonus of knocking and walking into any of our friends' homes without waiting for an answer. So, once I arrived, I assumed my usual always-welcome posture and strode right in.

And it felt great to be inside, except that nobody seemed to be home. And the house was chilly, as always, even though somewhere a furnace was running. Still, standing in the vacant foyer in my as-yet-to-be-seen leg warmers, I was not easily put off. In fact, I was thinking about just staying bundled up, sitting down and waiting for my friend and her family to return—a practice that was far from unheard of—when it occurred to me to check the upstairs. Often, when their parents were gone, my friend and her seven siblings would hang out in the four bedrooms on the second story. *They might still be here!* I thought, and opened the door to climb the stairs. And that's when life changed.

Strangely, my transformation came in a very quiet moment; there was an absolute absence of thunderclaps or lightning. I did not see or hear from God. I just found myself standing in front of a woman I had known most of my life: my friend's mom. This was the same woman who declared me "nice" looking, and for years my four siblings and I had each had a friend among her incredible brood of eight. She was friends with my mother. She grew her own herbs, wore her hair in a bun, and baked rosemary breads so fragrant that the whole street could smell them cooking. And she looked, for all the world, like she was freezing.

She sat on the bottom step, leaning forward with her elbows propped on her knees. She had a blanket wrapped snuggly around her shoulders and held a cup of something hot in her hands. It appeared that she had closed herself in on the landing in order to warm herself over the one large vent meant to heat the entire upstairs. Having spent numerous nights there myself, I knew that this process often failed. I also knew that my friend's dad did manual labor, that her mom stayed home, and that eight was a whole lot of kids. Oddly, though, this was the first time that all those factors added up to equal "poor" in my mind.

I probably stood there for a second, dumbfounded. I don't remember what she said to me, although I know that we spoke. She probably told me, as she had a million times before, to come back later. She may have said my name. I do remember leaving and walking home. I was disappointed and confused: My friend hadn't seen my new clothes, and I had seen her mom in a way that seemed somehow more private than if she'd been naked. I was embarrassed and felt strange because I had never had to find the one warm place in my whole big house and then curl my young self around it as greedily as I had just seen a grown woman do.

And while I know that my small realization may seem like something far short of a revelation to most people, it is how I came to know that I wasn't poor. I was just a girl with a pathetic wardrobe (new leg warmers notwithstanding). And I already knew that I wasn't rich, despite my ability to swim in my own backyard. Instead, my family and I existed as so many others did and still do: in the strange and shifting ether of the middle class. For a preteen kid, though, it came out much more simply than that. No, I wasn't swathed in gold, and my backpack had been my sister's. But was I warm enough? Yes, I was. Almost always.

A Privileged Path in a Class-Shattered World

ANNE ELLINGER

I'm about eight years old, waking up in my New Jersey bedroom with the purple-and-blue tulip wallpaper and the violet gauze curtains. These sweet sounds wake me up: first, my dad shaving, the water gurgling down the drain, the swish of his shaving brush, the *scritch-scritch* of the razor across his face. And second, a Strauss waltz from *Der Rosenkavalier*, our family's current obsession. I always awaken to classical music. I jump out of bed, run past my dad in the bathroom, and jump into bed with my mom, where we snuggle and listen to music until my dad jokingly swats me out of bed to get ready for school.

This ritual, which I breathed in morning after morning for years, is my touchstone for the love and nurturance that filled my childhood. The giant trees that lined our suburban streets, the safety to walk unescorted to school a half hour away, even in first grade. Long summer evenings playing pretending games in the cool grass.

What is class privilege, and what is good luck? Certainly many well-off families are violent, abusive, alcoholic, or just plain mean. My family not only had plenty of money but was astonishingly functional. My parents got along. They loved us. They loved their lives. Sure, my mother was beside herself trying to raise my peculiar middle brother (I was the youngest of three). Sure, in my young adulthood I realized that my parents hadn't a clue how to deal constructively with conflict, so growing up there was a wordless family pact never to express anger. This had its cost—but minor compared to the profound benefit of being deeply loved and secure, the bedrock that supports me now, every day. How much of that is class, and how much my family?

When I was eleven, in 1966, my family traveled to India. I remember being surrounded by children my age begging for a *pisa* (a hundredth of a cent). "Why can't we take them all home?" I pleaded with my parents. My response to injustice and class oppression has always been like this: gut-level, immediate, and unreasoned. It just seems wrong! It's simply wrong for some people (of which I'm one) to have way more than they need and some people to have far less than they need! This problem should be fixed! Most of the last forty years I have struggled to reconcile that primal reaction with the glued reality of the world-as-it-is and to find my niche in nudging society toward a more equitable direction.

In my teens and early twenties, as the movements of the sixties and seventies raged around me, and my awareness of injustice deepened, my main reactions were guilt and dissociation. Intellectually, I was learning more and more about starvation, brutality, impending nuclear annihilation, overpopulation, racism, genocide. . . . But close around me all was peaceful and beautiful. I felt swaddled in a suffocating cocoon of comfort. (I lived in Honolulu during much of this time, caressed by gentle trade winds scented with flowers.) Like many privileged young people, I berated myself relentlessly: What right did I have to complain about *anything* in my life when I was so lucky compared to most? No right. And what was I doing to right the wrongs? Not enough, never enough.

To make matters worse, when I turned twenty-two my parents obliviously handed me $20,000 from a trust they had set up for tax purposes a decade before. No guidance, no strings. The money—which could have covered ten years' worth of living expenses for me, at the rate I was living—only intensified my shame about class privilege and my confusion about how to earn a living. I stewed in guilt. I felt especially confused in my early thirties: by day I was getting to know and love angry public-housing tenants (via my organizing job, where I facilitated heaps of meetings in smoke-filled rooms), and by night I was getting to know and love angst-filled millionaire inheritors (at posh conferences where I listened to the woe of drowning in money and purposelessness). I was a bewildered visitor on two different planets.

Little did I know that all that pain about money and class was preparing me for my life's work. As I now see happens for many people, the area of my greatest difficulty became the area of my greatest contribution. But I had a lot to go through between inheriting that money at age twenty-two and starting More Than Money (a peer support network for inheritors) with my husband, Christopher, at age thirty-four.

Some of what I needed to learn—what I and my politically righteous friends all needed to learn—was that the world is not so black or white, so all or nothing. All rich people aren't the bad guys, all poor people the good guys. Nor vice versa. Earned money is not inherently virtuous, nor is inherited money evil.

I recall a class-conscious friend declaring she would never set foot in our house because it was bought with inherited wealth. Years later she softened her stance and even chose a life partner with inheritance. I recall that when Christopher and I bought that house with my best friend and her sister, we were all so intense about what was "fair" given our different economic circumstances that it took us five years of heated meetings to write our co-ownership agreement. Decades later, we're still friends and cut each other a lot more slack. We needed to become gentle with each other, to understand that the choices any of us make personally about money and class are not so earth-shatteringly important. Yet as we softened, we needed to stay true to our core beliefs: that how we behave collectively, as a society, around money and class *is* important and needs deeply to change.

Over time, I developed this philosophy, which I found clarifying. There are aspects of "class privilege" that really should be the rights of all: clean air and water, economic security, self-determination, meaningful work, good health care and education, to name just a few. When I'm ashamed of those privileges or hold back from enjoying them, I don't help anyone; only working to assure their broader access helps. Other aspects of "class privilege" really should be allowed to no one: the power to exploit others, to destroy natural resources, to waste, to assume your way is the only or best way, to be oblivious and arrogant. To call these very different things by the simple name "privilege" obscures their profound difference and frequently stirs up paralyzing shame instead of motivating action.

In the first category, I've tried to share my comforts and delights in ways big and small: from welcoming neighborhood use of our hot tub, to sharing our home with lots of housemates, to loaning money (carefully) to friends, to helping organize a gorgeous renovation of the previously run-down park at the end of our street. I take time each day to appreciate the beauty and safety I get to live in and to remember those who don't. In the second category, I work to help others wake up and share their wealth. I also try to remember that the thing about oblivious and arrogant rich people is that we're oblivious! No doubt that includes me.

How much is enough—to give, to keep, to do? I still don't know. Sometimes I'm at peace with my choices and feel proud of the role I've played. And sometimes I still want to scream and scratch away the privilege that still coats me. Making our way in a class-shattered world . . . it's a never-ending dance.

Oreo? A Black American Experience

JOHN VAUGHN

At an early age, I was introduced to the idea that an "Oreo cookie" was sometimes more than just a sweet treat. For blacks, it was a phrase used to describe someone whose race was black but whose values and orientation were white—black on the outside; white on the inside. I learned about the concept of "Oreo" when I was being teased about being one. It hurt. I did not want to be an Oreo. I wanted in the worst way to prove that I was black, but felt that somehow I did not know how. Was there something that I should do? Did I have to talk with an attitude? Did I need to wear certain Afrocentric clothes? What was the secret to acceptance? My mother's constant refrain was "be yourself."

In February 1994, my mother, a psychology professor at Holy Cross College in Worcester, Massachusetts, asked me to speak to her class on the Black Family about my African American experience. Her class had just finished reading Ellis Cose's *The Rage of a Privileged Class: Why Are Middle-Class Blacks Angry? Why Should America Care?* In preparing my presentation, I read the book. The combination of reading the book and preparing for the class opened a floodgate of experiences and emotions that I had long forgotten and stored away. Feelings of rage, shame, and embarrassment were unleashed, along with waves of repressed memories, many of them unnerving. I was poignantly reminded of the challenges I faced growing up as a black American male in predominately white circles.

Many of the whites I knew saw black people and black culture as a monolith; they saw no diversity in the black experience. They saw no class differences or cultural distinctions. Their view of black people was that "they" were poor and lived in public or subsidized housing, they spoke Ebonics, seemed to have an unwarranted chip on their shoulder, and were lazy and not as smart as whites. But I did not fit that frame—my house, neighborhood, school, church, and my parents' leadership roles in the community didn't fit the image. Yet the long-forgotten phrases coming from the mouths of white peers and friends included "You don't talk like a black person"; "Are you on scholarship here?"; You live in *that* house?"; "Why are black people always so angry?"; and "Why don't they just get a job and take care of their houses?" The lack of media portrayals of class diversity within the black community certainly helped to reinforce these daily messages.

Worcester is a predominantly white working-class city, and I was conscious of class from an early age. Class was expressed by the neighborhood in which you lived. We lived in a middle-class neighborhood; most of our neighbors were either just taking the first step out of the working class or were already solidly there. Schools were another big indicator of class. Private schools were where the wealthy kids went; public schools were more working-class and middle-class oriented, and the Catholic schools were a mixture of everyone. I went to private school through ninth grade. I then attended a local Catholic school where I was one of two black kids amid a campus of almost a thousand kids.

I experienced race and class as synonyms. Black = poor. If you were black and not poor, you were the exception. I lived in a house that was bigger than most everybody else's house whom I knew—two floors, a backyard, and a finished basement. My stepfather's passion was working on the house and yard, so not only was it a big house, but it was the best-kept and nicest house on the block. All the neighbors had great admiration of our lawn. We were experienced as not being like other black people.

For my white peers, I was not like other black people, for I lived by the rules and values of the dominant white culture. In my white world you didn't talk directly about race. Occasionally someone would make a comment about blacks, but the tag line was always, "John, not you, you're not like that."

My father was in a doctoral program in physics at Boston University when he met my mother, who was in a doctoral program at Clark University in Worcester. When I was two years old, he died. After my father's death his insurance enabled my mom to buy a house and send my brother and me to private school. Eight years later, my mother married my stepfather. He was a Jamaican immigrant who was very entrepreneurial—he started his own courier service. In fact, over time, my mom and stepfather invested in at least four real estate opportunities, including the house I grew up in. They understood the value of investing in real estate as a means of building long-term equity. I have continued, at least in part, this tradition in that my wife and I own the New York City co-op in which we live.

The importance of a good education was another one of the values I inherited. We have the good fortune to send our kids to private schools. When we looked at New York City public schools, we saw a school system that does not perform well, particularly for black boys. We decided that the tradeoff of a good education, even if our sons would be among the few blacks in their schools, was one worth making. My wife and I both had the experience of being one of very few black kids in our schools growing up. We believe that we can help our sons manage the challenges and take advantage of the opportunities before them. Once you are on the right educational "train," you're in good shape. We believe that our sons will have choices as to where they want to attend college.

Growing up I absorbed the values of the world in which I lived—a mixed-class white world. One of the values I learned from white working-class culture, which my stepfather shared and embraced, was the importance of hard work, an entrepreneurial value. I also learned the value of a good party. My parents were very social, and we had lots of parties at our house. There was much food, drink, music, and laughter. What I remember most was that these gatherings were really diverse, from my mother's mostly white colleagues from the Psychology Department at Holy Cross and racially diverse friendships in the local community, to Jamaican newcomers to the United States sponsored by my stepfather, along with local businessmen that he had known for years. My parents were bridge builders; they helped bring diverse people and communities together. Retrospectively I can see that they were building a cross-class and cross-race community. Other values came more from my mother's professional middle-class world—taking pride in being black, the importance of a good education, involvement with social clubs, and the importance of civic engagement. (My mom has always been actively involved in the local community. After she retired, she served for ten years on the Worcester School Committee.)

Growing up, I spent a lot of time with whites in school and at church and was generally an accepted and valued member of those communities. My struggle was with my underdeveloped sense of racial identity and its integration into my whole self. It was a struggle that made me feel separate and not rooted in the everyday experiences of black people. One of the unspoken (and sometimes spoken) values I learned was not to be "an angry black person." In fact, economic security and social acceptance hung in the balance. The "angry black" didn't get the job or the promotion and was deemed ungrateful. If you wanted to move up the class/economic ladder, you couldn't be angry.

In looking more closely, what I at times experienced as racial difference was actually more about class difference. At times I felt different from other blacks because of class. In the wider black community there was not a lot of mixing across class lines, and I ended up in a whiter world. Among whites I was supposed to represent black culture. I remember being in a grammar school music class, and the teacher saying to me, "John, you'll know this song since it comes out of the black tradition." I didn't know the song, so I felt like I wasn't a good black person.

I did not rock the boat and never challenged situations when I felt treated like an outsider because of race; since my class was similar to the whites around me, I learned to be quiet and listen. The only person I ever talked to (and not even much) about my feelings about not belonging anywhere was my mother. I remember one time our high school basketball coach gave a pregame pep talk, and it ended with, "Let's get out there and beat those niggers." I was speechless. The co-captains of the team tried to support me by telling me he didn't really mean it. This incident epitomized my experience of being, as Ralph Ellison said, an "invisible man." Quiet = invisible.

Luckily, we had a strong, black extended family in Worcester that was composed mostly of other middle- and upper-middle-class blacks who spent a lot of their school and church hours in white communities as well. We spent most of our holidays and special family celebrations visiting with each other. Connecting to other blacks of a similar class felt like being home; I had a sense of comfort and connection, a sense of ease. I didn't feel the outsiderness. I could bring my whole self into the family. As I got older I valued my extended family more and more.

When I began speaking to my mom's class, I shared with them my initial feelings of guilt, shame, and "otherness" at seemingly not being part of the black community. I grew up in the 1960s and '70s when "black was beautiful." Black youth had posters of Martin Luther King Jr., Malcolm X, Bobby Seale, James Brown, little Michael Jackson, and Jimi Hendrix adorning their walls. Dashikis and jewelry with the black power symbols were worn by those who were serious about being black. However, although I knew these people and symbols, they were not central to my life. I wasn't familiar with the black-identified phrases and colloquialisms and oftentimes felt lost in conversations among some blacks outside of my extended family. There were many occasions where the way I spoke made me stand out. Black junior high and high school peers would tell me that I spoke like a white person. I knew very little about the world of black music and musicians. I grew up being tutored by "rock and roll." My closest friends were white.

I felt the most embarrassment and shame because I unknowingly began to internalize, but never verbalize, these dominant messages. Maybe I and my extended family were the exceptions; maybe "real" black people were a monolith; maybe black people and poverty were synonymous. Maybe all those negative messages were right.

My existence was a paradox between what I was being socialized to believe about black people and the diverse black community I actually experienced through my extended family in Worcester, as well as Washington, D.C.; Louisville, Kentucky; and Montego Bay, Jamaica— the places where my mother, father, and stepfather were raised. I struggled a lot with not wanting to be seen by others and myself as an "Oreo." I wanted to prove to everyone, and myself, that I *was* black on the inside. It was not until I entered seminary that I began the journey toward more fully understanding and claiming the diverse reality of the black community and claiming my own identity as a black American male.

When I spoke to my mother's class, I was reminded of an insight that it took me years to fully internalize—there is no single black American experience but many black American experiences. All black Americans no longer live in the same neighborhoods, as under segregation. We are no longer rich and poor living together, but are more spread out and dispersed. The perception that there is one "black community" and one "black community experience" is a fallacy, often perpetuated by whites as well as some blacks. The black community is as diverse as its white and other counterparts in culture, class, and experiences. My life is no less of a black American experience than that of a black person from Washington, D.C., Atlanta, Chicago, St. Louis, Birmingham, Oakland, or New York City. I am a black American, and this is my experience.

For the longest time I knew I was not alone in this journey, but I certainly felt alone. It was not until I reached adulthood that I fully understood in my soul that I was not the only person who had this experience. There are others who have walked and are walking this journey. There are others thinking or feeling that they are the only ones dealing with this experience. *This essay is for you.* It took me a while to claim and embrace my black American experience. I hope that in writing this, I help others to do the same.

Class Is Always with Us

KYLE HARRIS

After devouring bowls of soup, Carolyn, Hillary, and I sipped homemade mead, waxed philosophical about social change, and condemned the violent deeds of rich white men. Soon the conversation turned toward personal debt. I bragged that I paid my credit cards off with a $9,000 check from the New York City Police Department, who had falsely arrested me during the Republican National Convention protests.

My friends appeared as impressed with my story as I was with myself. I had lived a lot with that debt: hopped from one summit to the next protesting capitalism, shot a feature film, wrote a novel, and spent copious amounts of time fulfilling my desires scot-free, thanks to those thug cops.

Soon the conversation shifted from my heroic pretensions toward Hillary and Carolyn's student loans. They discussed their struggles paying debt on grocery clerk wages. I listened, fearful they would ask the dreaded question, and before long, the inevitable occurred.

"How much more do you have on your college loans?"

A class-guilt bomb exploded in my gut. How would I get out of this one?

Mostly educated in private school, I often felt the sharp contrast between my middle-class identity and my fellow students' wealth.

Rarely did I experience the awkward feeling of my privilege exceeding others'.

My first day at the Pembroke Hill School, kids gloated about vacations to private islands, horse-riding lessons, and eight-week summer camps. All I did that summer was play in a muddy creek across the street from my house and hide from Missouri humidity reading Mark Twain at the air-conditioned library. Dumbfounded, I began my journey attending private elementary, middle school, high school, college, and graduate school on my parents' dime.

Carolyn and Hillary were busting their backs paying for four years of public university, and I was about to bust my heroic pose.

"My parents paid the loans," I said. Instead of leaving them with my sheepish declaration, I justified myself. "Well, see, Grandpa was a coal miner, and my grandma worked as a waitress in a small Appalachian town. Grandpa died when Mom was seven. As a single mother living on tips, Grandma put Mom through college. That inspired Mom to pay for my education, which has been amazing. I didn't grow up rich. My parents just prioritized education over other things."

True, but kind of smarmy.

In second grade, the year before my parents sent me to private school, I remember a kid looked at my house and said, "It's a mansion."

By Liberty, Missouri, standards, I grew up rich. No doubt about it. I had food, comfort, even luxury; vacations; golf, swimming, and ballroom lessons; and buckets of toys. My parents and I ate popcorn at the Cineplex, bowled at the local alley, and attended concerts, symphonies, ballets, and an opera.

Mom, Dad, Grandma, and I lived in a house large enough for fifteen adults. Mom liked that it was big and white, just like the president's. She felt successful when Grandma hollered "whoooooo-eeeeeeee" and grinned a false-teeth smile. Having grown up poor, Grandma loved oversized houses, nice furniture, and as many luxuries as my folks could afford. Dad enjoyed painting, repainting, carpeting, and wallpapering Mom's personal Smithsonian.

Growing up I never thought much of the house, the enormous quantity of food we ate, the brand-new Buicks, the eighteen Christmas trees, or the gas-guzzling cross-country road trips. Despite so many luxuries, my parents lamented how teachers earned less than other professionals. Listening to them, you'd think we were poor.

Only when suffering through conversations such as the one with Hillary and Carolyn did I feel bad about having it so damned good. That night my two friends saw through my act and talked between themselves. I sat listening, ashamed, wishing I had pulled myself up by the bootstraps, knowing my political arrest at the RNC, my police-paid loans seemed downright trust-fund-crust punk compared to their paying off their debt sacking groceries.

Shortly after that night, a guy who worked retail at a Big and Tall Men's store asked me out for drinks. He spent our date insulting Jews, calling his only black friend "Token," and referring to dykes as "carpet-eaters" and "bitches." Later that week, disgusted with myself for groping a bigot, I left a cowardly message on his machine. "Uh, I don't want to go out with you again. I don't want to go out with Archie Bunker. You're seriously racist, and I just don't have time for this."

The next morning, I woke up to his calls.

"How dare you call me Archie Bunker? I'm no racist. I'm no sexist. I love people of all races. And at least I don't live in a basement and ride my bike to work."

Archie Bunker trashed my dignity attacking two key signifiers of my progressive nonprofit class status—my bike and my basement. How could he?

Indignant at the speck of class bias in his eye, I failed to remove the twenty-ton tree trunk lodged in my gaping pupil. In trying to combat his racism and sexism, I flaunted my private-school perception that being working class caused his bigotry. I had called him Archie Bunker—Hollywood's stereotypically backward, racist "average Joe."

My private schools taught me to avoid racist and sexist epithets. While my peers' parents exploited global labor and lived plantation fantasies eating feasts prepared by underpaid black servants, these modern-day slave masters never used racist names. Their mannered language buffered them from acknowledging their white supremacy and helped them feel superior to the redneck, Ku Klux Klan, Wal-Mart-shopping, factory-working, wife-beater clad hicks, the "real bigots." These rich phonies, who recoiled at the "N word," whose kids called me "white trash" and "faggot," waged war against poor people and people of color under a color-blind guise. Their attitudes laid the groundwork for my critique: my date was not simply racist, but just one more uneducated, working-class racist, a regular Archie Bunker.

For years I resented my parents for throwing me into private schools, cesspools of wealth. Because of my folks' liberal leanings and commitment to public education, their decision seemed grotesquely hypocritical. In response to the privilege they bestowed upon me, I rebelled and listened to Confederate rock and country music, dipped tobacco, drank whisky, and wore more flannel than Paul Bunyan. At the same time, I developed antiracist politics, fought skinheads and cops, and decried the prison industrial complex, racial profiling, and police violence in black and Latino schools. I performed white trash antiracist anarchist to the best of my ability, attempting to cleanse my class privilege in a baptismal stew of anticapitalist activism, defeated southern sympathy, and a love-hate relationship with the big box stores that my private-school peers disdained for all the wrong reasons.

To this day I identify with rebel cultures. Whether it's punk, hip-hop, country, or grunge, I've blistered my hands clinging to class rebellion, trying to climb my way out of the pit of wealth that defined my education. In my escapism, I tell myself I'm not unlike historically notable leftists: Che Guevara, Roque Dalton, Peter Kropotkin, and Vladimir Lenin, all of whom spent considerable energy fleeing wealth and uniting with the working poor.

Mom instilled in me the taboo against publicly discussing money, to protect me from those who had more and those who had less. I'm sure Lenin's mom tried the same. From coming out queer to admitting I no longer believed in God, I've struggled hardest to confront the money taboo, to acknowledge the economic conditions that shape me. Doing so leaves me vulnerable to critique, ridicule, and most frightfully, honest dialogue about what I have that others do not. And thus I ridicule myself, caught up in tiresome guilt most anti-oppression activists reject as a useless exercise in sly egoism and self-pity. My story ends. I stand at the center of the debate, clinging to class privilege through bitter irony, private-school delusions of grandeur intact, fancying myself in the ranks of famous leftist militants.

PART IV

Owning Class

RICH. AFFLUENT. SUPERRICH. WHOM DO WE consider wealthy? Like many class terminologies, there is no precise marker or measure.

In recent years, we've heard about the 1 percent versus the 99 percent. But even this generates confusion. The top 1 percent of income earners earned over $600,000 in 2010. The top 1 percent of wealth holders had net worth over $6 million. While there is a high overlap between the top 1 percent of wealth holders and income earners, there are many households with high earnings but also high expenses and little savings.[1]

We choose the term "owning class" because if refers to people who own substantial wealth, not just those who receive a high income. With this concentration of wealth often comes intergenerational wealth and power.

The owning class includes people who are first-generation entrepreneurs who have accumulated substantial wealth in their lifetime, usually through business ownership. But it also

---

1. Lisa A. Keister, "The One Percent," Duke University, 2013, http://www.wealthinequality.org/uploads/Keister_-_Annual_Review_ of_Sociology_-_The_One_Percent.pdf.

includes those with inherited and family wealth going back several generations. For instance, Jennifer Ladd is a descendant of Charles Pratt, who made the family fortune in oil and joined the board of Standard Oil in the latter half of the nineteenth century. Chuck Collins's family's wealth came from his great-grandfather Oscar Mayer, who started a successful meatpacking plant in the 1890s.

As inequality has grown, the share of income and wealth flowing to the top 1 percent and 5 percent has increased. Between 1983 and 2010, nearly three-fourths (74.2 percent) of the total growth in household wealth in the United States accrued to the top 5 percent of households in wealth distribution. Meanwhile, households in the bottom 60 percent saw their wealth decline.[2]

In these essays we hear about the blessings and challenges of growing up with privilege, money, private schools, good health care, and other opportunities. Our contributors are people who wrestled with the advantages of money and social capital while holding the American values of equity, justice, and fairness.

Chuck Collins relates his experience of growing up in Michigan during the 1967 Detroit riots, when he became even more aware of racial and class inequities and how his family was different from others. He describes the elite private school that he attended with Mitt Romney and how he lost perspective about where he fit into the U.S. class system because he was surrounded by kids from relatively wealthier families. He points to the ways that social policy and tax law have protected his family's wealth over generations.

Catherine Orland describes the nature of privilege as she experiences it—struggling with a sense of superiority, with assumptions, with her own attitudes and beliefs while she works to be an ally to working-class people. Orland commits herself wholeheartedly to making this world a better place despite her class background and all its baggage.

Sarah Burgess shares how talking about money was not done in her family because her parents believed children should not have to worry about money. But she does worry and finds herself grappling

---

2. Lawrence Mishel, Josh Bivens, Elise Gould, and Heidi Shierholz, *State of Working America*, 12th ed. (Cornell University Press, 2012), 376.

with complex emotions connected to having privileges without working for them herself. Burgess describes her process of learning about money, her place in the society, and how class adversely affects her and others through guilt and shame—to have such privilege without working for it herself.

Jennifer Ladd describes her owning-class childhood and her awareness of its advantages. In her "old wealth" family, she had the privileges of vacation homes and enrichment experiences of music, camp, and inherited wealth. Instead of feeling paralyzed, she makes thoughtful choices about how to act in a world of extreme inequality.

Charlotte Redway describes a day in the life of an owning-class person, as she begins her day working as a therapist with economically struggling young families. Then she heads off to meet with a financial planner about her investment holdings. She deeply feels the complexity of crisscrossing the class spectrum several times a day.

Sally Gottesman describes the role of social capital and "access" in her life in the form of powerful people who shape public opinion or people in positions of power and decision making. She also reminds us that, yes, money provides access, but "money can't buy you love" or even significant social change, all by itself.

Some readers may be surprised or perplexed by the pain and guilt expressed by several of the owning-class contributors. "Guilt is my companion," writes Sarah Burgess. "I worry about embodying the entitlement and elitism that are stereotypical hallmarks of my class." Catherine Orland expresses the pain of realizing she has "gained at the expense of others."

The experience of unlearning privilege requires a deepening of empathy. Expressions of guilt and shame, as described in this section, are a healthy response by people awakening to the pain of the class system. Various emotions get labeled as guilt. Some guilt is paralyzing or triggers a reverse resentment. But other feelings of guilt should be welcomed as a human response to the pain and disconnection that exist in an extremely unequal society and world. Guilt, properly channeled, is a motivation to take constructive action, to take responsibility for making the world right.

Born on Third Base

CHUCK COLLINS

On my first trip to downtown Detroit, fifteen miles from my home, I realized I lived in an entirely white world. There was not a single nonwhite student in my public or private elementary school. In our suburb of Bloomfield Hills, the only black people we saw were women at bus stops. They were maids returning home to Detroit after working in the suburbs.

ON A MONDAY MORNING in late July I detected an unusual buzz of conversation in my house. My father wasn't going to work that morning. He was on the phone with his employees. I kept hearing a word I didn't know: "riot."

The previous Saturday night, the Detroit police force, which was mostly white, had raided an illegal after-hours club and arrested eighty-two black people. A riot had erupted. The city government had imposed a news blackout on Sunday, something unimaginable in today's Twitter and instant cable news world. We didn't hear about the riots until Monday morning.

On Monday afternoon, the *Detroit News* arrived with enormous headlines and pictures, and the TV evening news showed dozens of torched buildings lighting up the Detroit skyline, looters breaking windows, and white police arresting scores of black rioters.

The riots continued all week. I started a scrapbook, with pictures of the riots I clipped from magazines and newspapers. Before the week was over, 43 people had been killed, 467 injured, more than 4,000 arrested, and more than 2,500 stores looted or burned. Three Detroit Tigers baseball games had been postponed.

I tried to make sense of the TV commentaries and snippets of adult conversations I overheard: "criminals," "crazy," "lawlessness." But my mother didn't use any of these words. "Why are people rioting?" I asked her, as she sat at the kitchen table, smoking a cigarette.

"Because they believe things are not fair," she answered with sadness in her voice.

"What is unfair?" I asked.

"That some people have so much and others don't have anything."

I paused to take this in.

"Do we have a lot?" I asked.

"We have much more than most people," she answered evenly.

My world got more complicated that morning. There were blacks and whites, those with much and those with little. There were people who were so angry about unfairness that they would riot and burn buildings in their own neighborhoods.

"Something is not fair," I said aloud. "It's not right."

"No," said my mother. "It's not fair."

My father returned to work in downtown Detroit. A few years later, he relocated his growing company to Ferndale, five miles outside the Detroit city line.

July 1967 was an important month in my life. I realized that my circumstances were very different from other people's. But many years passed before I began to grasp the enormity of the gulf between Detroit and Bloomfield Hills, that it was one of the hugest wealth gaps in the country.

LIVING IN BLOOMFIELD HILLS, I was soon absorbed into the white and affluent cushion of my surroundings again. The next time I had a jarring sensation of separateness—of how different my family was from most others—was when I started a new school in third grade, Brookside.

For my first three years of schooling, I had attended a local public school, Vaughn Elementary. My teachers had been dedicated older women, their lesson plans firmly rooted in the 1950s. Vaughn was a good public school in an affluent suburb. Learning was happening, even though my second-grade teacher had to manage twenty-five kids. Our day was structured around standing in line and proceeding in an orderly way to and from lunch, recess, and our buses.

Like at many public schools, the cafeteria at Vaughn doubled as the gymnasium, with long tables that folded up to make way for afternoon dodgeball games. We stood in line to collect our food trays and cartons of milk and pay a lunch attendant with little red tickets. The all-purpose room had no windows, but bright fluorescent lights ensured we could distinguish a chicken finger from a cheese stick. The din of children's voices echoed throughout the cavernous hall, and after fifteen minutes, we had trashed the room—spilling milk, throwing Jell-O, and mashing Tater Tots into the floor. Lunch monitors, crabby women in white aprons, dispensed threats and reprimands.

On my first day at my new school, I entered Brookside's lunchroom in search of a lunch tray.

"Chuck, you will be at that table with the new students," said Mr. Beer, the second-grade teacher, pointing to a wooden chair at a sturdy table with place settings for eight. Natural sunlight flooded the lunchroom through a bank of windows, and colored stained-glass chandeliers hung from a peaked wooden ceiling. One hundred students filed in, the only sounds soft murmuring voices and squeaking shoes.

Just as I was about to sit down, I noticed all the students were standing behind their chairs. The room became completely quiet. One teacher led a simple grace, and everyone joined in. After "amen," everyone pulled out his chair to sit down. Two students from our table sprang toward the kitchen, fetching platters of food and pitchers of milk.

Mr. Denio, the headmaster, sat at the head of my table. He wore a long brown suit jacket and tie.

"How is your first day going?" he asked.

Everyone politely responded "fine" and "good"—except me. I sat in stunned silence. Brookside didn't seem like a place where you could cut loose at lunch—no catapulting Tater Tots over to the girls' table. In fact, there were girls at my table! Vaughn hadn't been so bad, I thought.

"Well," he said, looking at each of us. "There are lots of new routines to learn, no?" We all nodded. "The first day will feel long. But you'll get used to it."

Mr. Denio poured us each a glass of milk from a pitcher. We carefully passed the platters of food. Our forks clanked on the ceramic plates.

"How old is this place?" I asked.

"Brookside was established in 1922," responded Mr. Denio. "Parts of this building were originally a seminary, where they trained ministers." Brookside had been started by the Booth family—wealthy newspaper owners—the William Randolph Hearsts of the Midwest. All the students and teachers were white. The tuition cost in 1967 was as much as a year at a private college, and there were no scholarships. Pressure to diversify changed this in subsequent years.

A brick tower with a balcony overlooked the small campus. The hallways, lined with leaded glass windows, were full of natural light. Sculptures surrounded the redbrick sidewalks. It seemed too nice to be a school.

Enrolling me at Brookside had been my parents' idea. They said it would be fun—and the classes would be smaller.

My third-grade teacher, Mrs. Warner, welcomed me and two other new students to our class of fifteen. The veteran pupils said hello and introduced themselves. Some shook my hand formally.

Our classroom door opened directly onto the playground. From my desk, I could see a geodesic dome climbing structure next to a soaring weeping willow tree. Swing sets, slides, and monkey bars stood on thick cushions of wood chips. Beyond them was a creek, the "brook" of Brookside. When recess time arrived, Mrs. Warner propped open the door. I waited to line up, but everyone else simply dashed outside.

In my first week, we were assigned to write a poem. Mrs. Warner praised mine effusively and insisted I read it aloud to the class. She also suggested that I submit it to the school literary magazine, the *Tower*.

No bells rang in the hallways, no teachers or grouchy lunch monitors yelled at us. Nobody had to line up. Mr. Denio was right: I could get used to it here.

ONE MORNING, my father dropped me off at Brookside, and I decided to wait until a familiar face showed up before walking down the path to school.

The courtyard where I waited was surrounded by brick buildings and tall hardwood trees. Across the street a low stone wall bordered more than three hundred acres of woods, pathways, studios, museums, and classroom buildings that made up the Cranbrook Educational Community. Almost all the Brookside boys continued on to middle and high school at Cranbrook and the girls to Kingswood.

A jet-black Town Car pulled up. A black chauffeur wearing a suit and cap popped out of the driver's seat to open the passenger door. Out climbed Bill Taubman. *He was rich.* His father, Alfred Taubman Sr., one of the nation's biggest shopping center developers, was among the wealthiest men in Michigan. We waved, and Bill walked toward the school. He wasn't the familiar face I was waiting for.

From where I stood, on a slight rise, I could look past an athletic field and the small brook to a mansion and gardens perched on another hill. The house belonged to my classmate Kathy Iacocca. She didn't need a chauffeur to bring her to school. She and her sister walked down the hill, through a gate, and across a little bridge linking the Iacocca mansion to Brookside. Her father, Lee Iacocca, was chairman of the Ford Motor Company.

A red Karmann Ghia pulled into the circle. The convertible top was down on this warm September morning. Out climbed Jimmy Nederlander with his book bag and a piece of toast. His father, James Sr., wore a leather jacket and sunglasses. The Nederlanders owned several professional sports teams, major theaters, and concert halls around Detroit. Jimmy was already an accomplished equestrian, winning medals for horse jumping at the Bloomfield Open Hunt Club. The Nederlanders were obviously rich.

At Brookside, the only class diversity I saw was a distorted micropicture of stratification among the very wealthy. Up until about age thirteen, I described my family as "middle class." I knew that the Iacoccas, Taubmans, and Nederlanders were clearly upper class. What I did not know was that we were all bunched together in the very upper triangle of a wealth-ownership pyramid.

Finally a familiar face showed up. Bruce Aikens was another kid just like me, not from a particularly famous or superrich family. For me, the connection to my great-grandfather Oscar Mayer was remote, like a faded photo, something having to do with my distant relatives, and none of my classmates knew of my family heritage. We walked down the path, sharing our nervousness about our coming day at school.

I HAD NO IDEA then that my family was wealthy, comfortably in the top 2 percent of the wealthiest families in America. But I had no perspective. In Bloomfield Hills most people were in the top 2 percent, and the only real class distinction we saw was between us and the uber-rich, those in the top one-tenth of a percent.

At Brookside and later at Cranbrook, I might crane my neck and look up the economic ladder, gawking at the kids in the top one-thousandth percentile. I might think of myself as only "modestly affluent" compared with them. And no doubt they considered me a diminutive player on the wealth "farm club" rather than a real major leaguer.

They were wrong. None of us could see the aerial view of the economic landscape. I was the fourth generation of an immigrant success story—of a vast fortune that had been started eighty years before. Nobody in my immediate family was famous or powerful. Our family fortunes had peaked, and we were just starting down the other side of the mountain. This was in part due to the simple mathematics of wealth dispersal among the expanding progeny. In my generation, there are ninety-six of us who are great-grandchildren of the company's founders, Oscar and Gottfried Mayer. The wealth dispersal was also the result of public policies after World War II, such as inheritance taxes and progressive income taxes.

These forces combined to scatter the great fortunes begun in the first Gilded Age after 1920. At the same time, public investment in educational opportunity such as the GI Bill, student loans, and housing moved the United States toward a widening white middle class. By 1967, our society was stumbling toward expanded opportunity, at least for white people.

My father grew up in a house of servants. I would not. Unless I could parlay my privileged position into some form of entrepreneurial wealth creation, it was unlikely that I would be as wealthy as my ancestors. The most likely scenario, under the rules of the 1960s, was that wealth would slowly dissipate like air from a tire with a pinhole leak.

But powerful social forces—what some call Reaganomics—would lift up capital and allow stationary wealth and assets to multiply fourfold in the 1980s and then fourfold again in the 1990s. The dismantling of the post–World War II social contract, the attack on unionization, and the tax cuts on capital would buoy the Brooksiders, expand our fortunes as asset inheritors, while betraying those whose economic security depended on a day's work and a paycheck.

Meanwhile, I rode on a multigenerational wave of privilege, a sense of security and well-being hard-wired into my life. I had a sense of belonging, of life with little economic anxiety, that past generations of economic insecurity could not undermine. This privilege included good health, thanks to quality medical and dental care, outdoor summer camps and recreation clubs, schools with sports programs, low stress, and family vacations.

My parents teamed up with other parents, taking turns employing each other's kids so that we could develop work experience. I did yard work and other chores, painted barns, trained dogs, and patched concrete walls. This helped me develop a work ethic, communication skills, and confidence, in a friendly lower-risk environment. These advantages, combined with social confidence, compounded as I moved into future school and employment situations.

I had won the ovarian roulette game. I was born able-bodied in 1959 into a white Christian owning-class family in the United States—a family that was riding a wave. I had hit the lottery at birth. Thanks to changes in government policy during the 1980s and 1990s, it would be a lottery that would keep paying out for the already wealthy.

Money Was Never a Worry

CATHERINE ORLAND

When I was growing up, money was never a worry. I never knew how much money my parents made until I was busy filling out the bubbles to apply to take the PSAT in the seventh grade. I was standing by the phone and working on our black marble countertop while Dad stood at the kitchen island, washing the salad for dinner that night. I asked my dad what our family income was. Without missing a beat, he responded, "What's the highest one?"

I scanned the bubbled choices and hesitatingly ventured, "150,000 plus?"

"Yeah, that's it," he said, his tone rather blasé.

Shocked, I asked him, *"Really?"*

"Yeah," he replied, and then almost as if he were taking offense, "What did you think it was?"

"Uh," I stammered, "I dunno. I guess I never really thought about it."

"You never thought about it!" Dad sounded incredulous. He had grown up poor, the son of immigrant parents, in Trenton, New Jersey. His father had been a union organizer during the McCarthy era and delivered milk. His mother had been illiterate. He spoke exclusively Yiddish in the home until he entered kindergarten. Dad and Mom had moved up only through education—through scholarships to affordable schools.

"No." I admitted. "Why would I have ever thought about it?" At this point my dad, probably feeling very far away from me on the class spectrum, said nothing, grunted, and continued to make the salad dressing while I went back to the bubbles on the PSAT application. That was an awkward moment of awakening to my own class privilege. I hadn't considered myself rich.

At my private school, most of us called ourselves upper middle class. After that day, I started thinking of myself as rich. I started understanding my own position in an entirely different way. I never again questioned which bubble I was supposed to darken. It was always "the highest one." The realization—that it had never occurred to me to think about my family's income—coupled with my dad's reaction to my naïveté, left me with many questions, most of which I'm still untangling.

While the benefits of growing up with money are obvious, the costs of privilege are harder to name. I find it painful, both to me and to others, how I have absorbed the elitist and warped attitudes of a life surrounded by wealth—attitudes that I still, oftentimes unconsciously, bring to people and situations. I constantly struggle with my own internalized class superiority. I constantly have to check my assumptions. I routinely evaluate my behavior. I trip all over myself by being classist on a daily basis. I am clear that my work around class requires me to see how my behaviors and actions are unjust, and to think, behave, and act in ways that work toward greater social justice.

I used to have many classist assumptions about what constituted basic education. For example, I thought that knowing how to use a map to navigate was something that everyone knew how to do. I realized later, however, that this was a skill my parents taught me when we took vacations—nothing I ever learned in school. I thought that knowing how to read and do simple arithmetic was pretty much a given. But that theory was blown out of the water when I landed a job as a public school English teacher, right out of my elite college, and was confronted with white middle-class ninth graders who couldn't read, sitting in *my* classroom.

Attending private schools from kindergarten to twelfth grade did little to prepare me for the emotional impact of the grave injustices faced by students who had simply slipped through the cracks. I was shocked and appalled. I suppose I could blame my ignorance on myself or on my environment, yet I had studied the concept of failing schools in college, so I had actually known about others' troubles, yet I had only engaged intellectually with these issues. In doing so, I kept myself at a comfortable and safe academic distance from "their" realities, "their" suffering. This allowed me to avoid feeling personally responsible for students who had been failed by failing schools and, importantly, I never had to critically examine my own role in perpetuating this unjust system.

I also blame the ways that capitalism shelters the rich from the ugly realities of poverty. Prior to teaching illiterate ninth graders, I was never personally touched by lack of opportunity and benign neglect—and I certainly had never seen my own educational path as tied to anyone else's. Even as I write this, I am aware that by blaming capitalism and the status quo for my ignorance about poverty, I am able to easily evade and avoid my own guilt. I'm employing a classic tactic for folks from my class background—to deny privilege and responsibility by blaming the system.

When I entered graduate school, I was surprised that I had classmates who didn't understand the words "meritocracy" and "hegemony." "Where did these people go to college?" was my first thought. It would take a whole year for me to understand that even my undergraduate education was not the norm. Liberal arts educations at small, elite colleges are reserved for the privileged few, and I was lucky to be among them.

My advantages came full circle for me when I worked for the public school system in Maryland. I was running a dialogue program in one of the most racially and financially diverse school districts in our nation, bringing parents, students, and teachers together to talk about the racial achievement gap in schools. At this time, I was also writing my graduate thesis, and it occurred to me that the entire process contained academic elements that were familiar to me. From the proposal, to the research, to the data collection and analysis, I recalled episodes in my earlier educational path (even a sixth-grade lesson about research skills using index cards) that guided my way. The contrast between my being able to grasp and succeed at a process that was new to me and the fundamental unfairness of the achievement gap—and those who are not given the skills to get to where I so "easily" have come—was stark. To further add to this contrast, my research topic, multicultural education, sought to eliminate the very achievement gap that I had benefited from. Ultimately, I found it somewhat incongruous that my elite private-school-based education had led me to learn about multicultural education—a field that aims to transform the public school system by giving all students the skills and the sociopolitical analyses that I received. The only difference is that my education cost $345,000 in tuition alone.

I now understand my place in the achievement gap and the wealth gap. I appreciate that in our current system, if some people are losing, others are gaining. As Tim Wise says, "If there are some people in this nation who are 'under-privileged,' do we not also have to assume that the inverse is possible? That there is also an entire group of people who are 'over-privileged'?"

In my case, I happened to be the one who gained and at others' expense. I always had a sense that there was something wrong with the privileges we received in prep school. I always believed instinctively that all the manicured lawns and the freshly planted flowers, the fancy cheese receptions and the thick carpets in the library, seemed excessive. I just didn't have the words or the courage to express it, and I certainly didn't have a forum or an audience for my thoughts.

On one hand, it was wonderful that at our high school we had access to a truly top-notch education. On the other hand, I always felt that it wasn't fair that we had so much when so many others had so little. Our teachers had advanced degrees from Ivy League schools and taught us to love learning rather than being bored by education. Our varsity teams traveled to games in plush private buses paid for by the school, passing by other teams who were holding car washes to raise money for their sports uniforms. Our uniforms, by contrast, were returned to us each game day, magically laundered and folded.

At the beginning of our eleventh-grade year, our class was administered a test with questions geared to help us choose the profiles of our ideal colleges. Throughout that school year we received comprehensive personalized college advising and assistance. They held our hand through every step of the process, helping us select low, middle, and reach schools, crunching the data on our SAT scores and grades, even editing and providing feedback on our admissions essays. When the time came for most of us to check off that little box—you know, the one that asked whether we would be applying for financial aid or not—most of us did not have to tick the box. The majority of my high school classmates had their college education paid for outright, free and clear, no loans. This is my story as well. I can think of no other example more lasting and profound than the privilege of not having to pay off school loans.

AFTER THE ECONOMIC MELTDOWN, our nation began to come to grips with the consequences of unchecked excess. Hopefully, some of those chickens will come home to roost. But I still wonder . . . what will it take for the elites to truly give? What kind of community efforts could inspire folks like me, and even folks who are better off than me, folks living in big ol' houses up on the hill, to willingly give that up in favor of a more balanced and equal society? At age thirty-two I am starting to see how easy it is to just think about me and mine, to want to do well for myself and make a nice life. But what gives me the right to comfort when there are others who are suffering and struggling right outside my front door? Oh sure, I can rationalize with the best of 'em, saying that my comfort and safety allow me to do the social justice work that I do. But really, let's be honest. That excuse just helps me sleep better at night.

I live in a really interesting and rapidly gentrifying neighborhood, the Mission district in San Francisco, which once was an Irish Catholic neighborhood and is now the last Latino stronghold of a city that prior to the gold rush was part of Mexico. Before that, the Mission was inhabited by the Ohlone people, who used Mission Creek, now a paved-over sewer, as a form of transportation out to the bay. I recognize that the vitality of our community, the artists and the murals, the small family businesses, and even the livelihoods of my downstairs neighbors, a Latino family who have lived in this building on rent control for fifteen years while our landlord neglects their slowly deteriorating apartment . . . that all of this is threatened by people who look like me, by people who have just moved into the top floor of a renovated Victorian apartment.

I am gentrification. I may not live in a condo (one complex is going up on the next corner) or drive an SUV, but I am white and educated. I have access to power, I know the right people, and though I still feel uncomfortable in old-money settings, I know how to act "proper." I have a set of behaviors and mannerisms that gives me access to power in this society. In addition to not having any debt, I have cultural capital. Though I certainly do not have a trust fund, or a lot of savings, I do have a safety net. If something bad happens, I know my dad would help me financially.

I make daily efforts to get to know my neighbors, to build relationships and community, and to support local businesses, but I realize that the ways I speak and the clothes that I wear cause other folks to decide who I am, and what I'm about, before they even give me a chance. Will that stop me from trying? I hope not.

My dream is a better world for everyone, and I stubbornly believe that we can get there if we just keep trying. I want to be a person who makes our world better. As I work for change, I ask working-class activists not to judge me for the privileges I have received. I don't need your anger at me, though I do need your righteous anger at the system. Above all, I need your patience and compassion as I work to examine and transform my role in creating poverty for others through my own success. This is not something that I, and folks from my class background, were socialized to do. I need you to be honest and to call me out and hold me accountable to my promises. Together, I know we can make change.

The Women Who Cared for My Grandparents

SARAH BURGESS

For me, class has been and remains intertwined with race. I learned I was wealthy from the black women who took care of my grandparents until their deaths. Anna and Ubalda, women from the Dominican Republic, cared for my grandparents in Washington, D.C. Sarah and Dorothy, women from across town somewhere, cared for my grandparents in Greenville, South Carolina.

These women were kind to me. Anna and Ubalda gave me and my brother presents for Christmas. Dorothy cooked us macaroni and cheese, ham and green beans. Sarah told stories. We greeted each other warmly whenever I visited. I hugged them; we smiled and laughed. I asked a little about their lives; they told me admiringly how I was getting bigger, growing up.

This greeting over, I would go out to the living room with my family while the women remained in the kitchen or another back room. I was aware in that transition of something askew. I felt, without clear words, that we had hired them to take care of us, that those were the terms of our relationship. It strikes me now that I also felt left out. I sensed that these women had other lives and selves that I could never know, even if I asked them to tell me about themselves or went with them to their rooms. I felt seen by them in a way that I couldn't see back, and this rift stayed with me. From then till now, one part of my experience of having money is a feeling of exclusion, a sense of separation from others.

I faced this further when I was older, at my grandparents' funerals. For the last three of them, I flew in from somewhere else to go to the ceremony. At my Washington grandmother's funeral, Anna cried and cried and cried. She said she didn't know how she was going to handle the grief. I sat with her, my tears small and light. I remember thinking that she knew and loved my grandmother as I didn't. She was with Nana every day, brought her breakfast and watched tennis with her on TV, combed her hair and brushed her teeth. I, meanwhile, saw Nana five or six times a year, around the holidays or when she came to watch me play soccer and act in plays. Mainly, Nana was lovingly peripheral. And so at the funeral I felt again left out, this time from a relationship with my grandmother.

I also remember wondering about Anna's family. Where were the ones who needed her, who knew her first and loved her deeply, who had history with her, whose ties were blood? And who would tend Anna so laboriously and lovingly when she was old and dying?

While the black women who cared for my grandparents taught me about wealth, I learned I wasn't poor mostly through absences. My parents never told me to get a job. In one conversation about summer plans, my dad said I would have plenty of time for jobs when I was older, so I should do other things. They never told me an experience I wanted—camp, travel—was too expensive. They never asked me to consider my college options in terms of cost. There were no late-night arguments about how to spend money, no discussions or preoccupations with saving and stretching.

As I grew older and started asking, my dad told me he hadn't talked about money with us because he didn't think children should have to worry about it. And I didn't. Not in terms of my health, my access to education, my overall sense of wellbeing. That is surely one of the greatest gifts of my life.

I did and do "worry" about it, though. Guilt is my companion. I feel shame about having what I didn't earn and spoiled by luxuries of choice and opportunity. I worry about embodying the entitlement and elitism that are stereotypical hallmarks of my class. I carry my worries in a chatter of judging thoughts, self-conscious about the way I move through the world. In my head, I hear myself reduced: "That's just because she grew up with money, because she doesn't know anything else, because she can't understand the realities of life out here where things are raw, where money grates on consciousness and dulls it, where striving and scraping and managing affect existence." And so I worry I have no place in making the world better, that what I offer lacks credibility and potency.

These worries coexist alongside a deep gratitude. Besides the experiences of the world that having money has afforded me, my class has allowed me to distance myself from materialism, which I consider a blessing. I do not feel like I have to prove myself through stuff, and so I am not particularly attached to it. My parents passed this on to me: our house is not big by U.S. standards; some of our furniture has shabby corners; appliances are likely to be old and shaky. My parents don't wear expensive clothes, drive fancy cars, or eat very fancy foods. I learned that I didn't need new things to define myself.

Over time, too, my relationship to money has changed. As I learn more about what I have, I feel more able to deal with it. I understand stocks, bonds, and mutual funds. I can speak with some assurance about capital gains and investment strategies. Through an organization called Resource Generation, I have been introduced to socially responsible investing, shareholder activism, and strategic giving. I am coming to terms with the cards I have been dealt and learning how to play them usefully. I am seeing more clearly how I can participate in creating social change. This learning helps dilute my worries.

But class still crops up in ways that unsettle me. Last night I spoke with an acquaintance about going to a conference. She told me she couldn't afford it. I can. I wondered whether and how to tell her that, to mention our difference. I wondered the purpose of doing so. I had wild thoughts of paying for her to go. I felt guilt. These moments happen constantly as I interact with others, assess my choices, and make decisions about my life. The sense of something askew that I felt in my grandparents' houses remains. The process of uncovering, understanding, and navigating the way class affects my life and my choices continues.

What Was It Like Growing Up Owning-Class?

JENNIFER LADD

I had a wonderful childhood in many ways. I grew up in Belmont and Cambridge, Massachusetts. My parents had professional jobs—university professor and psychiatric social worker—but both of them and their parents had come from legacies of wealth made in the late 1800s.

I experienced a lot of freedom. I was able to play outside with friends most of the time I wasn't at school, except for the acting classes and flute lessons. We lived in a comfortable three-story house, with each one of us four children having our own room, and with a basement big enough to roller skate in. Our family went skiing on weekends in the winter, hiking and camping in the spring and fall, and boating in an old converted lobster boat in the summer. When I was in fifth grade we bought a second home in Vermont, which we used year round.

I was able to attend sleep-away camp for two months where I learned to swim, canoe, sail, row, hike, ride, square dance, weave, milk cows, grow food, collect chicken eggs, and butcher chickens for food. My siblings and I were sent to child-centered, private schools where we learned academics along with woodworking skills, music, painting, and pottery. We went to school with the children of Nobel Prize winners, ambassadors, famous authors, conductors, professors, and politicians.

Our family traveled during school vacations to places like Florida, the Virgin Islands, and Mexico, where my father did archaeology with Harvard University. Later, during high school, I traveled around Europe on a moped with a group of friends. When we were home we enjoyed museums, the theater, and skating on surrounding lakes.

How incredibly lucky. Yes, and I am grateful for it. I did gain tremendous knowledge, experience, and affirmation growing up. Yes, there were issues of divorce, death, and depression that have left their mark as well, but every family has its challenges.

Along with all these benefits, I was also fortunate to grow up with awareness that not every child has access to the education, travel, and lessons that I had. This awareness developed as a result of the historical period and the place where I grew up, accompanied by my parents' values.

I came of age as the 1964 Civil Rights Act was passed. Being in Cambridge and Boston I was surrounded with love-ins, the first Earth Day, and marches against the Vietnam War. I was immersed in the values of equity, justice, caring, and human rights and yet clearly lived with more than others because of the family I was born into.

I remember one incident in high school that brought out this societal unfairness and my feelings about it. I went to a small private high school in downtown Boston housed in a brownstone on upscale Commonwealth Avenue. By the time I was a senior, the school was integrated with low-income students, both people of color and white people, from low-income and working-class neighborhoods like Dorchester, Mattapan, and Roxbury.

Our school was dedicated to a strong scholarship program that brought people from the ends of the class spectrum together—an unusual happening, considering how segregated schools were (and are) because of real estate values and bank policies.

Each year, the senior class would traditionally go away for the weekend to celebrate. I offered our house in Vermont. Our school had only about one hundred students at that time, so our class was around twenty-five. The house was a former farmhouse. It wasn't fancy, but it was spacious and equipped for all seasons.

I was very glad to share this large space with others. It was a great place to play in and around. But I was also self-conscious about having not only a whole other house, but also one that was so big, with two barns, a smaller house, and so much land.

The senior class carpooled our way up to the house in Vermont, and my fellow students ooh-ed and ahh-ed about what they saw but soon dispersed to enjoy the pond or jumping in hay in the barn or going for a hike.

There was one student that I was most nervous about. He was African American and came from Roxbury. He didn't speak often and sat hunched over. I interpreted the way he acted, thinking he was angry, resentful, and that he didn't want to be there but his parents had made him come. I was imagining that he felt alienated and that he hated being at this house in Vermont, which shoved in his face what he didn't have.

Later that afternoon I overheard him say something about a "rich bitch" living here. I thought he said it loud enough for me to hear. His comment hit me in the solar plexus. I felt like an object, the enemy, and a person to be abhorred. He had voiced my biggest fear. I left immediately and hid under the porch while I cried my eyes out.

I so didn't want to be seen as part of the rich and powerful that we were all so busy protesting and critiquing—and yet that is the heritage and reality I came from. I thought I understood his point of view; part of me shared a sense of outrage at a society that has such wide wealth disparities, where many live in rundown apartments with absentee landlords, and a few others have multiple homes.

The boy and I avoided each other for the rest of the weekend and really for the rest of the final semester, though the school did host some very honest discussions about what it was like for those students from the low-income parts of the city to come to this private school in an upper-class part of Boston. Some of the students talked about the challenges of living in two cultures—the school culture and their home culture. I learned a lot from listening to them.

Later that summer I headed off to college, where my sociopolitical education continued and class differences in the larger society manifested themselves in the course of a strike supported by the low-income and upper-class students that shut down the school. The strike was broken with an injunction brought by a group of middle-class students who couldn't afford to lose an expensive semester of college.

After college I moved with friends to Dayton, Ohio. I was working as a social worker, particularly with very low-income African American elderly people, most of whom were struggling to make ends meet. Many had been house cleaners and caregivers who had never received Social Security for their work because domestic workers were not eligible. At the same time I inherited almost $1 million.

At first I wanted to give it all away—to get rid of it. Those I knew who had inherited wealth said, "Fine, give it away, but do it thoughtfully." I decided to set up a small fund that supported groups in Dayton and Cincinnati. I didn't want to be the sole decision-maker, and I didn't want to abdicate my responsibility either, so I invited other community workers without money to participate in choosing the grantees.

I, like many others, have felt the pain of living in a society with such extremes of wealth and poverty. I, like many others, have searched for an appropriate response that faces that pain, while appreciating the true value of what I have and who I am, without cringing with guilt or shame. Now I do what I can with the money, time, attention, and passions that I have. Taking action to create a thriving, sustainable world with whatever resources we have seems like a mandate for us all.

A Day of Traveling across the Class Spectrum

CHARLOTTE REDWAY

Traveling across the class spectrum is for me, at this point, both exhilarating and exhausting. Let me paint a picture of a Monday morning. I arrive at work at 10 a.m. for a staff meeting where we, all family therapists, have an hour of "check in." I work with a fabulous group of people, including a thirty-five-year-old woman who over the last few months has been sharing her incredibly difficult time worrying about her brother. He has taken to the streets and is "using" again. My coworker struggles as she tries to get him into the same treatment programs that she advocates on a daily basis for her clients to get into. It's different when it's family.

My "check in" this week is about my weekend at my mother's. I came away from her place frustrated by the vastly different relationships we have to the family's wealth. As I share this story, I fidget with the fear of my colleagues judging me or thinking sarcastically, "Oh, poor rich girl." I begin to elaborate on these fantasies in my head, convinced that they are determining how unfit I am for this work—how could I, a "poor rich girl," adequately provide family therapy to multi-stressed families living in the crisis of poverty? I feel removed and as though I am distancing myself from my coworkers around me. At the same time I trust that my story is important and my colleagues have known me long enough to respect my struggles and my work.

I finish speaking, and my thirty-five-year-old colleague turns to me. "My brother is really smart, you know, and although he's on the streets, he's doing research. He's studying why people give him money. He's really curious about this and asking lots of questions. He wants to know what leads people to help. You give a lot. I bet he would love talking to you. Would you be willing to talk to him?" I tell her that, absolutely, I would be willing to talk to him. I am relieved to be an accessible person with wealth.

I leave the staff meeting to go meet with a family to provide family therapy. At the end of the time together, the mother pulls me aside and tells me, "You are the only service provider I like." I ask her why, and she tells me, "Because you're not rich, like the others." At first I feel complimented, and then confused. And then ideas of professionalism, self-disclosure, and boundaries step in. I want to tell her that, in fact, I do have a lot of privilege and wealth. I'm tempted to get up on my soapbox and say, "There are good rich people," but this is her time, her therapy, and I fear that bringing all of this into the room would be making it my agenda instead of hers. For this reason, I simply say, "What do you mean?" and she says, "You talk like me. You dress like me. You're not like them." I am resistant to any totalizing "us/them" discourses but leave the comment be, aware of the incredible power differential at play. My limited awareness of her context allows me to accept this as a compliment.

I go from this meeting to an appointment with my financial adviser, where I ride the elevator up to the fourteenth floor and then sit in a leather chair, being offered coffee as we discuss stocks while overlooking the river. I feel underdressed. I feel out of my league. I don't feel like trying to fit in. Instead of becoming self-conscious, I decide to make a plug for the families with whom I work. I ask my financial adviser to make a donation to them. She agrees, and I am amazed by how easy that was to talk to her about helping out.

I leave my financial adviser to go join a woman who has just left a domestic violence situation and is trying to get TANF (Temporary Assistance for Needy Families) in order to support her children. She has been sitting in the welfare office for half an hour by the time I get there. We've agreed that if I'm there to advocate for her, she's more likely to get help. We sit for four hours in the welfare office with her two children before her name gets called, and even then, she gets turned down for assistance. She heads off to catch the bus back to her mother's, and I get my car from the parking garage.

Two blocks out into the city lights, I pull out my cell phone with the intention of calling my friend. There is a message blinking, so I listen. It's my attorney calling again—more papers to sign, accounts to manage, decisions to make. I dial my friend's number. She answers immediately. "I have rich-person whining to do," I say as soon as she answers. "What do you mean?" she asks. "Today was weird" I say, frustrated at my lack of descriptive words. "I'm tired. All the shifting between worlds, it's exhausting. Why do I do this to myself?" I tell her the story of my day, and she reminds me of the values I have shared with her over time, the importance of connection, the exhilaration of being that bridge.

Social Capital

SALLY GOTTESMAN

Many, perhaps most, mornings when I turn on the radio to listen to the news, I feel disheartened and disempowered. The news is bad and getting worse. I am tempted to turn the radio off and forget about all that is going on "out there." After all, what difference can I make? Who'd listen? At least in here I can play "music class" with our three-year-old and one-year-old and know that my voice makes a difference.

But then, sometimes, I catch myself and ask a question that I believe it is incumbent for me to ask: "If I don't think I can make a difference, who does?"

Why do I ask this? In part because it is a variation on a question raised by Hillel, a Jewish sage who lived in the first century BCE to the early first century CE: "If I am not for myself, who will be for me? If I am only for myself what am I? And if not now, when?"

But I also ask it because in more lucid moments I remember that I have access to people with power in our system. Not that I've earned it, but I was born into a family with money.

How does this translate?

I am writing this article at my family's office on a cold, snowy day in New York City where I am waiting for a meeting with someone whom I am interviewing to join the board of my family's business. When I Google him I discover not only is he a partner in a major U.S. law firm (I knew this), but he is also the chair of a major national not-for-profit organization. Later when we meet and I query him about this interest, he speaks passionately about the work of the organization, and he also lists some board members who are household names in the arts, history, and finance. Access.

As I write, my father walks into the room. My father, who grew up working class, went to college for free at the U.S. Naval Academy, and he has delivered a world of access to me. He asks me if I want to come in and meet my New York state senator who is coming to see him in order to raise money for his campaign for attorney general. I ask myself, "Do I want to chit-chat, or is there something I'd like to raise with him?" Access.

And earlier today I checked in with my friend who occasionally writes for the *New York Times* about an article idea I pitched to her about a Jewish meditation center in Brooklyn that I care about. And speaking of the *New York Times*, on Sunday good friends of mine ask me, did I read their good friend's column this week? Access.

If I think carefully about it, I believe that I am probably one or two degrees away from being able to reach a group of Americans with a certain type of power. Not that they'd do what I want . . . but I could figure out how to have access to them. And access is definitely a step in the right direction.

The most important access I ever had: when our daughter was six weeks old and needed an operation, my partner called a family contact, and within hours we had the head of a major American teaching hospital telling us who should operate on her in New York City and then contacting the pediatric surgeon, telling him to expect and take our call. I am eternally grateful for this and wish it could be so for everyone. But I'd trade all of my access to household names, senators, *New York Times* writers, and doctors in a second if this would make my daughter healthy. But this doesn't seem to be the deal life offers. Not for me, nor for anyone.

So what is access about in a more abstract sense, if it can't make one's child healthy? (Rule number 1: access ≠ miracles.) Access, whether because one has money or status because of one's profession (judges, senators, Nobel prize winners, etc.) or because one is partnered with or the child or parent of someone "famous," often means someone will return your call. And in a "knowledge economy" where we are inundated, this counts. It can help you to achieve your goals—to invest more wisely and make more money, to get the inside "scoop" on a topic of interest, or to ask someone to do the thing that you want.

Money—and access—can buy certain things. There is no doubt in my mind that people with money get undue influence with politicians. I know this because I give money to some PACs, and thus I am invited to speak with politicians. I could do this as an American citizen, but I can do it with much greater ease as a "donor."

Money, it should be remembered, can't buy love. I remember in my twenties realizing that I had, relatively speaking, a lot of money. I remember asking myself, What would be the joy in collecting things, even Fabergé eggs like magazine magnate Malcolm Forbes does, if one can always use one's money to purchase them? So I decided then to collect autographed books written by real friends.

Absolutely a collection that can't be bought.

So back to access and the morning radio, the world outside of my own particular concerns. I do think that it is incumbent upon me to be active and not "give up" because I do have access in a way that many others don't. Even if the problems feel—and are—beyond anything one particular person with or without wealth and access can change, I know that I must play my role in the causes I care about *also* using my wealth and my access. This is what I can bring to the table, and saving my access and money won't do anyone any good. This I am sure about.

PART V

Mixed Class

FOR MANY PEOPLE, CLASS IDENTITY DOESN'T FIT into a tidy box.

Some had parents raised in very different classes, so they were exposed to a variety of class sensibilities in their immediate family. Others were born into one class where they grew up and then moved to another country or community where the class structure was very different. Still others have experienced the roller coaster ride of both upward and downward mobility.

People whose parents came from the far ends of the class spectrum, very poor and very privileged, hold the dynamics of class division within their own families—and often within their own psyches. They may feel constant interior friction, as well as social discomfort, as they negotiate the cultural norms of each side of the family.

Mixed-class people can be especially good bridge people across class cultures. Some bring a capacity to see class issues from multiple points of view, thanks to having grown up identifying with different class backgrounds. They may be familiar with the intricate ways that class— all across the class spectrum—weaves through our daily lives.

Having a mixed-class background means one can draw on the strengths of each class background, developing working-class resilience as well as a class-privileged sense of possibility. One can also acquire the demons of each class, such as shame about growing up poor or wealthy. In some of these stories, the authors grapple with antagonism toward their upper-class backgrounds, wanting to feel more identified with the oppressed part of their family, rather than the more privileged part. But true healing seems to come from finding and synthesizing the strengths gained from each class background.

This part includes four mixed-class stories, written by younger authors between eighteen and thirty-seven years old. Writer Jacques Fleury explores what it is like to cross class and borders. Like many immigrants whose class drops precipitously when they move to a new country, his family is privileged in Haiti, but in the United States he is regarded as poor and lower status.

April Rosenblum describes growing up poor, with parents from different class backgrounds who have chosen an activist life in a poor community. Their choice of voluntary poverty has both limited her options *and* expanded her possibilities.

Contributor Zoe Greenberg describes living in a world of ideas often found in upper-class worlds, while only being able to afford to live in a three-room apartment with five other people.

Mariah Boone talks about her experience leading a Girl Scout troop and the starkly different culture and class norms of behavior between girls of different backgrounds.

These mixed-class stories make it clear that class is not just about money, but also about cultural and social capital: the knowledge, contacts, and cultural references needed to have power in the dominant society.

Coming Clean

APRIL ROSENBLUM

Lying in bed in my apartment, nursing my baby, I fall asleep for a few instants. When I awake to the sound of birds, people outside laughing, and golden light twinkling on leaves outside my window, I'm jolted back a few decades into a drowsy memory of the neighborhood I grew up in.

There was a time when my childhood summers felt this safe and carefree. But by the time I was eight, the crack epidemic had come to our Philadelphia neighborhood. Two different houses behind us were firebombed. Gunshots became a nightly occurrence in our back alley. Adults in our neighborhood struggled with addiction and got mixed up with the law, and kids around me grew tense. We were the lone white family in a black neighborhood, so we drew a lot of attention—especially from those looking to let off steam. Our front door got forcibly smashed in while I sat beside it; my father spent months repairing it. Kids threw rocks at my baby brother in my mother's arms.

Our neighborhood didn't give us safety, but it did give us freedom. My parents could afford to be full-time activists because they owned their own home, bought half-abandoned for a few thousand dollars. They were coming from two very different places: my father from an upper-class, intellectual family and my mother from a working-class family that skirted poverty. He willingly entered a life without money in order to spend his time on social change. She went to college, but I think she felt far more comfortable living on scarce resources with my dad than she would have been attempting to rise into the middle class, struggling to fit in and being judged by people with money.

Our lifestyle had been my parents' choice, but my brother and I didn't really have a say in the fact that we were growing up poor. We had very little money, no health insurance, and all secondhand clothes. We craved the foods and toys that other kids had, the stuff we saw in commercials. But our class position wasn't so straightforward. We had *resources*: intangibles from my dad like confidence in my thinking and belief that I could achieve big things. I think when you grow up with money, as he did, thinking big comes more naturally. Both my parents valued learning highly, and our mom, who didn't have to work, was able to fully involve herself in our lives and help us succeed in school.

Being white was something else I had on my side. Through the absurd twists and turns of white privilege and desegregation, I—but not my black neighbors—got to go to a public school in a wealthier area of the city. Unlike the schools our neighbors had to go to, mine was safe from drug deals and shootings.

It didn't feel all that safe to me; I got pushed around physically and verbally, and I got called ugly and poor. I remember trying to stand out of sight, in corners, where it wouldn't be so visible that my secondhand clothes fit poorly and emphasized all the awkward places in my body.

All of this gave me an excellent motivation to try to blend in as best as possible with the middle-class people around me. And with my white skin, I had a good chance at it—if I could just figure out what I was supposed to be copying. I remember deciding as a second grader to change my low-class-sounding Philadelphia pronunciation of "water" to sound like the blond midwestern girl who had transferred to our school, and the revelation I had in seventh grade, that all it took to look middle class was to match colors in your clothes.

By the time I was out of middle school, I had mastered some parts of fitting in with the middle class. I could pretend up to a point. But I could never feel at ease. I still couldn't bring people home with me. Compared to the houses of my middle-class friends, my house seemed broken down and irredeemably dirty. It felt easier for me to avoid knowing people well enough to invite them over than to risk letting them see inside.

Even though I kept my house out of sight, I didn't feel clean. For me, being poor felt like I carried with me a layer of grime that I couldn't ever wash off. On some level I really believed there was always something dirty about me that other people could see, even if I couldn't.

Yet every day when the school bell rang, I returned home to a reality that tilted all this upside down. Kids I played with had moms in jail, or they were having their first babies by the time I was off to high school. When I had trouble with kids around us, my mother counseled me to try to have compassion for them; I had it so much better than they did, they were bound to be resentful.

Although in dollar terms what we had was fairly average for our neighborhood, our racial and cultural privilege and our education made us seem so incongruous that rumors circulated that we were millionaires. To make sense of what we were doing there, people had to picture us as the kind of misers, or do-gooders, who choose to live in poverty versus living off their millions.

And really, I was as confused as they were. I felt rich compared to other kids when I was at home, but humiliatingly poor when I ventured elsewhere. The reality of who I was changed according to who was seeing me and what context they knew me in.

It took me many years to find a place where all my mixed-up pieces fit. Then I got into political activism as a teenager, and suddenly I was just one of a whole community of people who shared my level of education but had no admiration for material wealth.

The house I moved into after high school was as rickety as the one I grew up in, except none of my housemates felt any shame about it. For many of my middle-class-born friends, poverty was a political issue, not a personal experience; crack addiction was something people joked about at parties, and installing new drywall was controversial because one of our housemates considered it "bourgeois." Despite the odd moment in which I felt alienated by such a comment, this community was amazing for me to be a part of. For the first time, I didn't have to pretend in order to fit in.

To be around all these middle-class people who didn't judge me was the beginning of a slow recovery. I gradually started to see certain things in a whole new way. One day in my early twenties, I looked around the home of a wealthier friend and suddenly saw that her house was clean *not* because she was more civilized than my family, but because the materials in her house were newer, more seamlessly installed, and, by design, easier to wipe down. The materials in my parents' house, on the other hand, would never be clean, no matter how many times we might scrub. They were old, porous, shot through with crevices that had collected dirt over time that could never be removed. Until that moment, deep inside, I had bought in to the idea that middle-class people were just better than me; that they were somehow inherently cleaner than I was or would ever be. They seemed to know intuitively how to be normal and presentable. They shared a language I just couldn't speak.

I am still learning how to stop pretending. Every year I feel a little bit bolder about just being who I really am. There's a lot I cherish about my own class culture. Poor and working-class people—my family included—are incredibly resourceful and creative, out of necessity. We value people. We don't take friendship lightly. We know how to be there for each other. And compared to my middle-class partner and friends, I'm far less likely to assume authorities are right. After all, how often do people in power have poor people's best interests at heart? I'm quicker to say what's on my mind and not tiptoe around for politeness' sake, and I'm more willing to take a risk and dive into a new life endeavor with my whole heart, without waiting until conditions are perfect, or staying paralyzed, weighing the pros and cons.

I *want* to be able to look clearly at the good and bad that I've inherited from my dad's upper-class side, too. But I have found that, coming from a mixed background, it's hard for me to take a good look at my privileges if I haven't taken time to deal with the pain that came first.

For me, the worst part about growing up without money is not feeling safe—not physically safe from the violence that happened all around me, and not safe to be myself around people with more status. But I don't think middle- and upper-class people really feel safe either. They can buy alarm systems for their homes and send their kids to schools free of violence. But they are still targets when they walk down the street—targets of resentment from people who have less than they do, and targets of crime from people who will do anything to get what they have.

During high school, kids from my neighborhood were in and out of jail. But many of the middle-class kids I went to school with—who should theoretically have had easier lives—were suicidal, had drug habits, or were put in mental institutions by worried parents. More money didn't give them fewer problems; it just made them turn their problems inward.

The longer I experience many sides of it, the more I can see that the class system we live with is a lose-lose situation for everyone involved. But nothing is going to change while the subject of class remains closed. All of us have our fears when we open up and join the conversation about class. But I can tell you: it feels really, really good to come clean.

Ferragamos

A Cross-Class Experience

ZOE GREENBERG

I have Ferragamo shoes. They say "Salvatore Ferragamo" in gold script on the inside sole, and they're made of black leather, with a gold plate at the top of the round foot that holds together a black leather bow. The pair I have are selling as classics on the Italian website for $395, but I got them at a consignment shop for $25.

I began to think about shoes when I was discussing this class anthology with my godsister, Nava. We grew up together in Mount Airy, a racially mixed and economically mixed neighborhood in Philadelphia. We both grew up in one-parent households, and we both went to our local public school. We were brainstorming topics.

"You're tired of telling the story of transferring from your local public school to the wealthy private school nearby?" she asked. As an introduction to the work I've done around class, I usually tell this story, and in its retelling and cementing of certain phrases, it has lost a lot of its meaning to me. But it is important to understand where I'm coming from, so I'll say it briefly. Until fifth grade, I went to my local public school, which was underfunded, overcrowded, and never had enough resources. In fifth grade I transferred on full scholarship to an elite private school, which had small class sizes, beautiful grounds, and nearly endless resources. No one seemed to be talking about the enormous differences in wealth that existed so near each other, but I couldn't stop thinking about it.

"Yes, I'm sick of that," I said. "I want to talk about my Ferragamo shoes."

"Your what?" she said. "Your what shoes?"

This is exactly my point.

In Chestnut Hill, the prosperous, preppy neighborhood in Philadelphia where I went to upper school, the process of finding Ferragamos is intense. The well-coiffed matrons (or their housekeepers) donate worn designer shoes to local consignment shops. The girls of Chestnut Hill are on a constant hunt for these shoes, which are hard to find, because short of death or serious economic disaster, women don't give them up.

I never knew what Ferragamos were until it came to my attention that my best friend wore them every day. She has both new ones and thrift store ones, and she wears them with fancy dresses, mostly, which are her preferred outfit for school. I borrowed them from her for various events, and I found them to be relatively comfortable, and unbelievably classy.

When I saw them in the window at a consignment shop in Chestnut Hill, I went in and bought them immediately. I don't wear designer clothes. Mostly I wear flip-flops and sneakers on my feet. But something about these shoes had caught my imagination, and I was transfixed.

I showed them to my mother, brimming with excitement.

"Wow," she said, because she is supportive even when she has no idea what something is. Then she proceeded to call them my "Tomigotchi" shoes, in a way that made it unclear whether she knew she had the name wrong or not.

I told my friend Scarlett about them, and she was satisfyingly impressed.

"Where did you get them?" she said approvingly, and then she went to the same store the next day.

When my sister saw them, she scrunched her nose. I had given them no introduction, but she pointed to them and said,

"Those are kind of ugly."

"Rosi!" I cried. "They're *Ferragamos!*" By clarifying their title, I was trying to explain that they could not, in fact, be ugly. My sister, who is the most talented person I know, and who could make something equally beautiful in about fifteen minutes given the right, or even the wrong, materials, was unimpressed.

My friend Julie told me about her own Ferragamos in response to my purchase.

"I had really pretty white ones, but then the heel broke off. So I took them to a cobbler, and he fixed them easily. And he told my mom these shoes would last until my daughter's daughter died. They're so high quality. Obviously I can't wear them very much because I don't want to get them messed up." I nodded understandingly.

It seemed everyone I knew had a class-appropriate response to my Ferragamos. Either they had never heard of them, or they had a prized pair they held at equal value to their grandmother.

Slowly, I realized my experience with Ferragamos was a pretty apt metaphor for my experience straddling different classes. My own family is overflowing with intellectual conversations, elite education, and owning-class expectations, but our bank accounts are not overflowing with money. I have a mom who is single and four siblings, and the six of us share a three-bedroom apartment. But because I went to private school, the majority of my friends come from upper-middle-class or owning-class backgrounds.

Sometimes this straddling of classes is a real blessing, because I get to experience the joys of multiple classes. I revel in Ferragamos some days, and I revel in briefly getting my own room on other days. Sometimes it's aggravating, because I can't always articulate to those around me what makes some experience or pair of shoes important.

Ultimately, it's the difference in the underlying realities, and not the difference in the reactions to Ferragamos, that is most important. I have to wonder—if a pair of shoes can have such a wide span of meaning to people across the class spectrum, how can health care, or education, or democracy itself mean the same thing to people on opposite sides of the wealth chasm? As a country, are we even in the same conversation?

Two different approaches to footwear don't necessarily matter, but living in separate realities from those of our fellow citizens has high stakes. When those at the very top of the wealth spectrum lead our nation, I don't think it's crazy to wonder whether they have a true grasp of the culture and values at the bottom of the wealth spectrum.

Having different life experiences and different approaches to the world is not the problem; the problem is if all our approaches are not equally represented in our leadership, and if one approach becomes the norm.

I have in no way reached a conclusion about the ultimate solution to differences in shoes and perspectives. But for such a though-provoking and elegant item, I really do think that twenty-five dollars was a bargain.

Girl Scout Green

MARIAH BOONE

Being the mother of a Girl Scout has given me a startling window into the world of class.

At the beginning of my daughter's kindergarten year, I called up the local Girl Scout council to start a troop. I took all the training and filled out the copious forms required to become a Girl Scout leader.

I started a Daisy Girl Scout troop of four little kindergartners at my daughter's preschool. Soon, a child from a nearby school joined the troop. I had lots of fun helping the girls earn their petals by learning about different parts of the Girl Scout Law. After kindergarten, all our Daisies became Brownies and went on to first grade at different public elementary schools. Our group formed the core of our Brownie Girl Scout troop, but other girls joined, mostly from my daughter's school or whose mothers were friends of mine.

In our new Brownie troop, I began to feel some class discomfort. We met at my house during those Brownie years. But our pleasantly middle-class home seemed poor compared to the houses of some of the other girls. It is an odd phenomenon how most rich people think that they are middle class and that people like me are, I guess, working class. Certainly, I knew better. Both my husband and I had college educations and stable jobs. I worked as a social work administrator, a position that paid as much as a schoolteacher's job. My husband worked as a volunteer coordinator at a local hospital.

Our combined salaries made us solidly middle class and even privileged, even if it didn't seem like it to our wealthier friends.

I found the whiteness and prosperity of our Brownie troop a bit disconcerting, considering that we live in a predominantly Hispanic community that is not very wealthy overall. Technically, any girl from the community can contact the council, and she will be referred to local troops like ours. But I never got one referral in all the years I was a leader. I wanted to recruit a more diverse group of girls, but I didn't know how to go about doing that without its seeming weird. One of the other girls in the troop had her cousin's half-sister join up for a while, and I was happy because this kid was more working class, and I hoped that we were moving in a more socioeconomically diverse direction; but she dropped out the next season, despite my efforts to help her single dad get her to meetings.

For years, we stayed a group of girls that was not very diverse—several wealthy kids with a couple of middle-class kids thrown in for good measure.

Even so, Girl Scouting was a great experience for our girls. They learned leadership and character and camping skills—and so did I. It was a wonderful three years for me. I took the troop camping when I was almost eight months pregnant with my second daughter, but I handed the troop over to another mom when my baby was born. Juggling work and motherhood has always felt challenging to me, and it is a lot harder when you have an infant. I stayed on the sidelines of my daughter's Girl Scout troop until she was in seventh grade and the baby was four and I knew it was my turn to get involved again.

Attending the meetings again to help with the girls' Silver Award process, I got to see a strange class clash that surprised me. Two girls attending private middle schools had joined our troop in the previous year. They were quiet and polite when compared to our other girls, but they didn't always attend the meetings, and they were easily overlooked in the face of the energetic and noisy girls who had been in the troop since Brownies or Daisies. In seventh grade, though, something changed. The council let us know about a small troop that was looking to join another troop because their leader needed a break. These girls, some of whom I had actually known from our preschool days, came to visit our troop and see what it was like. Their parents came, too.

Suddenly, we were seeing our girls through other eyes—the rather disapproving eyes of private school parents. The Girl Scouts from the private school came into focus as a distinct group—just as confident and capable and funny as our girls, but also polite and able to sit still and be quiet when adults were talking. Our girls, by comparison, behaved horribly. They never stopped moving and talking and laughing—and yelling and singing and interrupting and arguing. It was humiliating. Our sweet leader was embarrassed, and I tried to take on my mean middle-school teacher persona to get our girls in line some, but they were unstoppable—a force of nature.

I think we had always enjoyed that about them before. But in the face of the civilized behavior of the new girls, and the disapproving-bordering-on-terrified looks of their parents, everything looked different. I was astounded. I had always been worried that our Girl Scout troop was too middle and upper class, our girls too insulated from people who had lived lives more representative of our community's true standard of living. But suddenly our original troop was a bunch of rowdy, scary public school girls who seemed like a bad influence. I knew that most of our girls, with the exception of my daughter, were as rich as the private school girls, so this class divide seemed odd to me. Was there really such a difference between the culture of the sort of posh magnet-type public schools our daughters had been attending and the culture of the private schools? Really? Apparently, there was. For a while, it didn't look like the merger would happen. Some of the private school moms were appalled by our girls. The troop leaders were determined to make it work, though. The girls didn't really like each other. The girls who had been in the troop the longest had been fine with the previous addition of the two quiet private school girls, but now, with the new girls bringing the troop into focus as two distinct parties, it was as though there was a threat to their territory. They said they were trying to make friends with the new girls but that the new girls didn't want to be friends, wouldn't talk to them. Attempts to get them to take the other girls' perspective or to see how intimidating their rowdiness might be to people who did not know them like their mothers did were largely unsuccessful. We had two troops in one and appeared to be stuck with it that way.

Then something interesting happened. A girl at my daughter's school joined our troop. She turned out to be a Girl Scout the private school girls had met at summer camp and really liked. Everyone liked her. She was working class, living with a single dad in a rough neighborhood and attending a grassroots evangelical church—the kind where you find lots of bikers. She was a lovely girl—not at all quiet, but not wild, either. She became a bridge. The private school girls loved her. The public school girls liked her fine. She brought them together somehow.

I still don't understand any of it.

Living beyond Class

My Journey from Haiti to Harvard

JACQUES FLEURY

My name is Jacques, aka "the Haitian Firefly" in artistic circles. I am a poet, author, columnist, journalist, and burgeoning novelist. I came up with the nickname "the Haitian Firefly" to reflect my bold individuality and life credo that we are all essentially fireflies; we glow only for a short amount of time, so we might as well shine as brightly as we possibly can while we still can.

I grew up in Port-au-Prince, Haiti's capital city, as part of a middle-class family. My father was an entrepreneur, tailor, and landlord, with his own business in Port-au-Prince. My mother and father never married, and they lived in separate houses. My mother lived in an inherited house with her four sisters after her parents passed away. My grandfather was an educated professional man who took great care of his family.

I lived in Carfou, an outskirt of Port-au-Prince, on Jean-Claude Duvalier Avenue. Even though my mother and her sisters were all educated, they still could not easily find work—that is, unless they were willing to compromise themselves sexually. And so eventually they all married money, professional men who could provide for them and afford them the luxury of living above the poverty line in the often precarious life of the middle class. I say "precarious" because the scale could tip below our favor at any time, which is exactly what eventually happened and caused us—me, my mother, and my stepfather—to leave Haiti essentially forever. We had lived in a two-story house with a pool in the back, very high surrounding walls, and rooms to spare. My mother rented out the extra rooms to tenants. She was given the title "housewife/landlord," a rarity for a woman in Haiti.

I first realized my position in society at the cusp of my adolescent years. One of my mother's tenants, a single mother with five hungry mouths to feed, helped me to see that I was lucky to have what I had. My mom would sometimes forgo this tenant's rent or feed her and her kids during particularly arduous times. Her kids sometimes studied on empty stomachs while I nitpicked about what kinds of foods I liked and didn't; and my mother would order the maid to cook me something else if I did not care for what was in front of me. I remember some of the tenant's kids scaring me into giving them my dinner by telling me that if I did not forfeit my dinner, the Ogoon (a Haitian voodoo king) would come and steal my soul while I slept. I succumbed to this trick for quite some time, until my cousin Bob persuaded me to retaliate and refuse to fork over my meals.

I felt very privileged when I saw the tenant's kids attending public schools while I attended a very exclusive private school, Frère André, adjacent to the Haitian White House. Back in the late seventies and early eighties, our family was the first to possess a telephone, a refrigerator, and a color TV, things that we all take for granted here in America. My stepfather would take my mom and me to the circus, the theater, and vacation spots like the Tropicana and Le Lambi, and he could afford us a lifestyle of fancy foods, furnishings, and leisure. However, being privileged came with a price.

My stepfather was an alcoholic mechanic with his own business, and while he provided us with luxury, he also inflicted grave suffering upon us. He was terribly jealous and possessive; my mom was not allowed to come and go as she pleased. She would have to be home before my stepfather came home. If she came later, he would drink, and it would erupt into a verbal and physical confrontation, from which my mom and I might have to run for our lives. Sometimes I would get physically hurt when I tried to separate them. Sometimes my mom would faint from being choked, and I used to fear that she would never wake up—a low-class price to pay for high-class status.

When my mom, my stepfather, and I landed in the land of the free, with the Statue of Liberty to welcome us, none of us knew what lay ahead of us. My mom told me just before we left Haiti that my step-father's business was failing and that our status would take a serious nosedive unless we left immediately while we were still on top.

When we arrived in Boston, we all had to live in a rooming house, in a windowless basement. I was only thirteen and found myself going to school wearing a multitude of motley-colored clothes that would later be defined as "the immigrant look." I discovered how comfortably other kids were living when I would go over to their houses. This made me yearn for the middle-class life I used to live back home.

One day, I came home crying to Mom, my chest heaving in emotional anguish, about how kids were teasing me for looking poor. They called me a "just come"—a term I later learned was reserved for people just off the boat who did not dress properly. (In actuality, our family arrived on a plane from Haiti with legal immigrant status.) A "just come" would supposedly do almost anything for a living at half the wage, perpetuating the myth that immigrants take jobs away from "real" Americans. My mom was patient, empathic and loving, a trait that has been consistent right from the day I was born. She told me to remember who I was before I came to America and not to let anyone define who I am.

As I became acculturated to life in America, I became more and more aware of how I was perceived and treated based on a number of factors. I am often perceived to be African American until I open my mouth and my persistent accent gives it away that I'm not from here. When I am perceived to be African American, certain stereotypes often go along with that—for example, that I like rap music, live in the 'hood, and speak improper English.

Another factor I found out could be used against me is that I am Haitian. The first thing people assume is that I must have grown up terribly impoverished, and then they assume that I must be their intellectual inferior since I speak English with an accent; but both these ideas are far from the truth. I did not grow up poor, and I also graduated Phi Theta Kappa Honor Society from college.

The stereotype that Haiti is an impoverished country is true; indeed, Haiti is deemed the poorest country in the Western Hemisphere. But what some Americans don't know is that Haiti is also the first black republic, the first free black nation in the world. They also don't know that Haiti boasts La Citadelle, the largest fortress in the Western Hemisphere, built under Haitian emperor Henri Christophe.

That I lived in poverty upon coming to America and that I come from the "ghetto" neighborhoods of Boston are true—however, that doesn't mean they stayed true.

Today I make a modest living as a freelance journalist and columnist for *Spare Change News*, the *Alewife News*, and from the sale of my book. I live in Cambridge within a mixed-class community, in my own apartment. I find that communication is the thing that stands between stereotypes and the truth, yet that is something people often neglect to do, because perpetrating maladroit stereotypes is easier than challenging lifelong misconceptions and prejudices. My worst fear is that when people see me, all they will see is a big black guy probably from the 'hood, undereducated, angry, and potentially a menace to society—none of which I am.

I used to be extremely defensive—and I still am to some extent—about the way I'm perceived. Being a black Haitian male in America has its drawbacks. I used to feel that I had to defend myself to anyone I perceived as giving me the slightest hint of negative judgment. Today, however, I don't feel quite so strongly about how others perceive me. Today, after having endured homelessness and stigma due to mental illness, then climbing my way out of the darkness to achieve my dream, I know that I am more than just an "unfortunate situation." I have also learned that sometimes what may appear to be, prima facie, an unfortunate incident may turn out to be heaven sent.

Back in 2003, when I was "unfortunately" diagnosed with post traumatic stress disorder, which brought with it the curse of clinical depression, I became homeless. I endured the shame and guilt of having to apply for government assistance. As a fifteen-year-old teenager, I started working at McDonald's. After high school and business school, I worked as an office manager, then as a health-care paraprofessional. I worked in human services as a residential counselor before I became ill and needed human-service assistance myself. But none of my work history kept me from feeling puny and "low class."

During the time of my illness and homelessness, I felt like "those people" I'd been warned about, as if being mentally ill and homeless were a contagious disease and that those afflicted must have done something wrong to put themselves in that position.

There is a Haitian saying, "Malady pa tombe sou pie bois"—illness doesn't fall on trees—meaning illness is the fate of all human beings, with an emphasis on "human beings." I saw the way people would look through me, as if I were invisible. Fortunately, my adversity beckoned forth my innate fortitude, a power bequeathed me by my upbringing in Haiti, that catapulted me like a meteor streaking across the sky to achieve what I thought was impossible, the American dream as it pertains to me: becoming a published writer.

I sought treatment for my illness, graduated with honors from college with a liberal arts degree, and started submitting my writings to local newspapers and magazines. *Spare Change News* gave me my first break. I also started to perform my poetry in the Boston/Cambridge area art scene and met book designer and burgeoning publisher Julia Henderson of Warbler Books. I have since published my first book, *Sparks in the Dark: A Lighter Shade of Blue; A Poetic Memoir*, about my journey out of Haiti, living in America, and achieving my American dream; it has been featured in the *Boston Globe*. I have also since been featured as a poet and author at many colleges and events, most notably the City Night Literary Series at Harvard University.

The pangs of class tension between myself and some of the people I come in contact with today don't bother me so much. My first major "aha" moment was during a recent conversation with my mom. I told her "Mom, I made it!" Ironically she responded, "You made it? You sure don't have the money to show for it!" I felt a little bit hurt, and I immediately responded with all the gentility I could muster. I said, "Mom, remember that you told me that happiness is about living and loving, working hard and being respectful to all kinds of people? I used to feel that you've worked all your life but don't have the money to show for it either. But you're happy. I once heard that if you want to change the world, do what makes you come alive. Well, I'm doing what makes me come alive. People write to me and tell me how my writing brings tears to their eyes and makes them want to become better people; that makes me happy, Mom. Isn't that enough?" She then said, "Yes, I guess you're right." And that was the last conversation pertaining to class and status I've had with Mom.

When I worked as a hospice nurse, one of my dying patients was a white man who happened to be a former Harvard University professor. As I held his hand until the end—me a black kid—he said, "You know, kid, at the end of the day none of this class and status stuff really matters. In the end, all that matters was what was true and truly felt and how we treated one another." An hour later he died, and I'm the better for having heard his final words.

Afterword

The Power of Story

BY CHUCK COLLINS

Class matters, as these stories show. Read together, this collection of stories has cumulative power and impact. Many of them still give me goose bumps even after I've read these contributions a dozen times.

I felt the shame Wendy Williams described when the cashier at the school lunch line knew she got the reduced-price lunch in spite of her best efforts to pass as middle class. I fumed with anger at the betrayals that Michaelann Bewsee felt at the hands of landlords and welfare officials. I delighted at the scene of Karen Estrella's taking her immigrant grandmother on her first and only visit to an art museum. I am envious of some aspects of Fisher Lavell's childhood, as she describes her mother's strong will and resourcefulness—or her father's, because when there was no meat to eat, he went out and hunted for their dinner. She always felt there was enough.

For the many "class straddlers" in this collection, I experienced, through their stories, how our class system made them feel bereft and like strangers in their families of origin, as well as in their middle-class lives. As someone raised owning-class, I empathized with Catherine Orland as she battled the judgmental voices in her head about privilege and shame.

These are the stories of our lives. They reveal the injuries of class, as well as the gifts of our various class experiences.

This collection dramatizes the woeful inadequacy of our class conversation and how little we really know of one another's lives. As wealth disparities grow, at the global level and within the United States, these differences in lives accelerate. We no longer occupy opposite sides of the tracks, but alternative and parallel universes. As distance grows, we lose opportunities to truly know one another across the class divide and hear one another's stories.

Story is a potent way to understand class and difference. Each story in this collection is unique, but there are prevailing patterns. At the universal level, we have all been dehumanized and held back by the class system. A membrane of shame appears to encase our experience of class. Sometimes it is as thick as mortar, other times it is thin as paper, with the possibility that it could be cast away.

A deeper understanding of class would greatly advance the discussion about race and white privilege. Race and class interact in powerful ways and cannot be untangled into neat categories. The importance of class has been racialized, and the conversation about race and gender differences has been distorted by class confusion.

If we fully understood how classist myths operate, we would be liberated from the limiting narratives of shame and blame that have been imposed on us by unscrupulous politicians, extremist pundits, and marketing moguls. And we could push back against the classist assumptions that are perpetuated in the status quo operations of our education system and popular culture.

Classist attitudes have deeply wounded each of us, with the greatest violence waged upon people living in poverty and struggling for material security. In December 2013, Pope Francis issued a powerful statement. Reflecting on extreme wealth disparities, he wrote, "Just as the commandment 'Thou shalt not kill' sets a clear limit in order to safeguard the value of human life, today we also have to say 'thou shalt not' to an economy of exclusion and inequality. Such an economy kills."

Indeed, imagine a world where the crude caricatures of class would not be tolerated, nor the public policies that justify extreme inequalities.

THIS ANTHOLOGY was initiated by Felice Yeskel, a beloved educator and activist, who edited most of the story submissions. Unfortunately, Felice died of cancer in 2011 and did not live to see this book published.

For me personally, the loss of Felice is a huge absence. She and I were close friends and collaborators for over thirty years, sharing a lifelong commitment to working against classism and inequality. We both became parents around the same time and loved singing to our daughters, Nora and Shira. Our two families had many adventures together, including several weeks traveling in Oaxaca, Mexico.

Felice and I had very different upbringings. Felice was Jewish, female, working class, and lesbian. I'm a straight white Christian guy who grew up owning-class, from a meatpacking clan. As we joked, together Felice and I were "Oscar Mayer Hotdog meets the Bagel Bagman."

Felice's key insight was that each of us holds a piece of the puzzle in the process of becoming human. She described how difference enriched us—how, for example, different race and class experiences give us complementary insights and information about the world. She didn't buy the idea that everyone should aspire to traditional norms of white middle-class culture. She knew how people who were raised poor and working class had tremendous skills, knowledge, and insight that come from their life experience. She fumed at how useful trades and working-class skills were undervalued, while phony wealth-creators and speculators were celebrated in our culture. In this context, Felice confidently reassured me that I could overcome the debilitating circumstances of my wealthy upbringing and that, with help, there was hope that I could develop working-class sensibilities.

As she wrote in the Introduction, "When we do talk about class, we tend to talk only about the strengths of wealth and the limitations of poverty. But in reality it's much more complex. All of us derive strengths as well as limitations from our class position and experience. Because of intense class segregation in this country, few of us have the opportunity to learn about each other's strengths and to grow past our limitations." The solution is building cross-class relationships and listening to one another's stories as we walk the path toward regaining our full humanity.

About the Contributors

MICHAELANN BEWSEE

Michaelann Bewsee is the longtime leader of Arise for Social Justice, a poor people's rights organization based in Springfield, Massachusetts, where she was born into a Catholic, working-class family in 1947. A single mother at the age of nineteen, Bewsee moved to Boston where she did clerical, factory, and waitressing work. She became active in communal living arrangements and social movements and cooked for the Black Panther Party's free breakfast program. After a period of homesteading in Maine with her partner, Bewsee moved back to Springfield. Her efforts, along with those of a few other women, to advocate for women on public assistance led to the formation in 1985 of Arise for Social Justice.

JIM BONILLA

Jim Bonilla is professor emeritus of organizational leadership and conflict studies at Hamline University in St. Paul, Minnesota. He has made more than five hundred presentations to schools, conferences, and organizations on the topic of diversity. Bonilla has served as past chair of the faculty advisory committee to the National Conference on Race and Ethnicity in Higher Education. He has spent nearly a decade as a community activist, first within the disability rights movement, and then working with low-income communities in upstate New York. Among his recent published works are "Making 'Green' Organizations Multicultural: Debunking the Myths about People of Color" and "Educating for and Assessing Cultural Competence." Jim is currently writing a book called *Navigating Destino:*

Five Lenses for Developing Cultural Competency. He now writes, consults, and stewards restored prairies and woodlands on a 149-year-old farmstead in St. Peter, Minnesota.

MARIAH BOONE

Mariah Boone is a mother, writer, teacher, social worker, and, of course, a Girl Scout leader. She lives in Corpus Christi, Texas, with her husband, two daughters, and three guinea pigs. She has been published in *Com-munityLinks*, *Off Our Backs*, *New Beginnings*, and various other print and online publications. Boone is the sometime publisher of *Lone Star Ma: The Magazine of Progressive Texas Parenting and Children's Issues* and writes a regular column on politics and parenting for *We the People News.*

SARAH BURGESS

Originally from Washington, D.C., Sarah Burgess currently lives in Philadelphia. After teaching for four years in New Orleans, she completed a master's degree in education at the University of Pennsylvania Graduate School of Education. Burgess combines her deep interest in education with her advocacy of progressive taxation to support public schooling in Philadelphia. She is also a member of Resource Generation, which supports young people with wealth who want to use their resources to support social change.

N. JEANNE BURNS

N. Jeanne Burns lives and writes in Minneapolis. She has been published in various literary journals and contributes to the Class Action blog, *Classism Exposed*. Some of her essays can be found in *Writing Cheerfully on the Web: A Quaker Blog Reader.* Her personal blog can be found at http://writeousnessjournal.blogspot.com/.

PAMELA BURROWS

Pamela Burrows was raised in a white upper-middle-class home in Philadelphia during the 1970s. She graduated from Macalester College in 1991 and has lived in the Twin Cities of Minnesota ever since. A Quaker with a passion for social justice, she blogs at www.rftlight.blogspot.com.

JANET CASEY

Janet Galligani Casey is professor of English and director of the First Year Experience at Skidmore College in Saratoga Springs, New York. She is the author of two prize-winning monographs, *Dos Passos and the Ideology of the*

Feminine (1998) and *A New Heartland: Women, Modernity, and the Agrarian Ideal in America* (2009). She is also the editor of *The Novel and the American Left: Critical Essays on Depression-Era Fiction* (2004) and *Teaching Tainted Lit: Popular American Literature and the Perils and Pleasures of the Classroom* (forthcoming). Other recent work includes co-curating a museum exhibition, with accompanying website and catalog, entitled *Classless Society*. She served formerly as the first senior chair of the Modern Language Association's Committee on Contingent Labor in the Profession.

CHUCK COLLINS

Chuck Collins is an organizer, storyteller, and activist working on issues of economic inequality. He is a senior scholar at the Institute for Policy Studies (IPS) and directs IPS's Program on Inequality and the Common Good (www.inequality.org). Collins is cofounder of Wealth for the Common Good (www.wealthforcommongood.org), a national network of business leaders and wealthy individuals concerned about tax fairness and shared prosperity. He has written several books about inequality, including, with Bill Gates Sr., *Wealth and Our Commonwealth* (2003), a case for taxing inherited wealth and preserving the federal estate tax. His most recent book is *99 to 1: How Wealth Inequality Is Wrecking the World and What We Can Do about It* (2012).

MONICA CRUMBACK

Monica Crumback lives in Michigan with her husband and daughter. Her essays and poetry have appeared in numerous publications, including *Brain, Child: The Magazine for Thinking Mothers*, *Super Faith*, *Skirt!*, *Referential*, and *Nailpolish Stories*. Trained in the Orton-Gillingham Method, she is a supervisor at the Children's Dyslexia Center of West Michigan.

JENNIFER O'CONNOR DUFFY

Jennifer O'Connor Duffy's research focuses on the intersection of gender and class in elite higher education. Her work includes "Invisibility at Risk: Low-Income Students in a Middle- and Upper-Class World," in the journal *About Campus*, and a book, *Working-Class Students at Radcliffe College, 1940–1970: The Intersection of Gender, Class, and Historical Context* (2008). With a background in college and university teaching, she has spoken nationally on the topic of how best to help working-class students succeed at college. She currently serves as dissertation chair at the Graduate School, Northcentral University.

ANNE ELLINGER

Anne Ellinger was raised upper middle class in suburban New Jersey. Her class awareness was shaped by two years at Movement for a New Society in Philadelphia and by having the bizarre fortune to fall in love with a millionaire. For more than three decades, she and her life partner, Christopher, have been helping wealthy people connect their money and their values: first through a national peer network and quarterly journal called *More Than Money*, and then with *Bolder Giving in Extraordinary Times* (www.BolderGiving.org). Ellinger is coauthor of *We Gave Away a Fortune* (winner of an American Book Award); the guidebook *Welcome to Philanthropy*, written for the National Network of Grantmakers; *The Bolder Giving Workbook*; and, most recently, *Getting Along: Skills for Life-long Love*. She and Christopher are passionate about performing Playback Theater with their troupe, True Story Theater (www.TrueStoryTheater.org).

KAREN ESTRELLA

Karen Estrella is a middle-aged, middle-class Boston suburban Puerto Rican woman who grew up working class in small apartments in New York and San Francisco. She now works as a doctoral-level expressive arts therapist and academic. She coordinates the Expressive Therapy track at Lesley University and has over twenty years of experience practicing expressive arts therapies and mental health counseling in community-based settings. Her most recent published work, "Social Activism within Expressive Arts Therapy: What's in a Name?" is a chapter in *Art in Action: Expressive Arts Therapy and Social Change*, edited by E. G. Levine and P. Antze.

SIERRA FLEENOR

Sierra E. Fleenor was raised in the Rocky Mountains of southern Colorado and graduated from Colorado College with a bachelor of arts in religion. She worked at Colorado College in student life where she received the Nelson-Cisneros Award in recognition of her work to support diversity, particularly around issues of class and LGBT rights. Fleenor continued her studies at Harvard Divinity School, where she completed a master's degree in theological studies. She serves as the Director of College Access and Success for the Colorado Department of Higher Education/Colorado Gear Up and works to implement better access to college for low-income, first-generation students. Fleenor attends the University of Colorado, Denver, where she is studying to become a couples and family therapist.

JACQUES FLEURY

Jacques Stanley Fleury was born in Port-au-Prince, Haiti, and now lives in Cambridge, Massachusetts. He is a poet, freelance writer, journalist, columnist, and novelist whose work has been featured in the *Boston Globe*, the *Boston Haitian Reporter*, and the *Somerville News*. He is the author of *Sparks in the Dark: A Lighter Shade of Blue; A Poetic Memoir*, about his life in Haiti and the United States. Fleury served as the official poet and publicity director for the Annual Urban Walk for Haiti to benefit Dr. Paul Farmer's Partners in Health. He is currently working on his first novel and has completed a book of essays and a short fiction collection.

SALLY GOTTESMAN

Sally Gottesman lives in New York City with her partner and their three children. A consultant to not-for-profit organizations in New York, she is the founder and chair of Moving Traditions, which works at the intersection of gender and Judaism to improve Jewish life. She has served on the boards of American Jewish World Service, Americans for Peace Now, and Congregation B'nai Jeshurun. Her articles have been published in *Lilith*, the *Jewish Week*, and *Sh'ma*, among others, and she is included in *Jewish Choices, Jewish Voices*. Gottesman was one of the women featured in the exhibit *Jewish Women and the Feminist Revolution*, curated by the Jewish Women's Archive.

ZOE GREENBERG

Zoe Greenberg is from Mount Airy, Philadelphia, and has been working on economic inequality since she was twelve. She is the writer and director of *Enough: A Kid's Perspective*, a short, award-winning documentary about wealth, poverty, and what is enough, which garnered her the Princeton Prize in Race Relations. She has presented her film and its accompanying curriculum at schools across the country and at the National Association of Independent Schools conference in New York. A recent graduate of Yale University, where she studied theater and English, Greenberg is contemplating a career in journalism.

KYLE HARRIS

Kyle Harris is an independent filmmaker, curator, writer, and instructor at the Colorado Film School. He received his master of fine arts degree from the School of the Art Institute of Chicago. His short films have won awards at the Chicago Underground Film Festival and the Sarah Lawrence Experimental Film Festival. In 2009, he and Kevin

Price founded Improbable Pictures, a social justice documentary production company. Together they are producing a documentary about the Underground Syringe Exchange of Denver and developing a documentary about the land-rights struggles of acequia farmers in the San Luis Valley of Colorado.

TIMOTHY HARRIS

Timothy Harris is the founding director of the *Real Change News* homeless newspaper in Seattle and has been active as a poor people's organizer for more than two decades. Harris has led numerous organizing campaigns on issues of homelessness, poverty, housing affordability, peace, and civil rights, and he teaches an honors course at the University of Washington on homelessness and poverty. He is a leader in the international street paper movement, a cofounder of the North American Street Newspaper Association, and a recipient of the Society of Professional Journalists' prestigious Susan Hutchinson Bosch Award for outstanding courage and integrity in journalism.

CAMISHA JONES

A writer, playwright, and poet, Camisha Jones has largely focused on addressing issues of poverty and empowering student leaders to respond to issues of inequality. After graduating from the University of Richmond in 1994, she spent two years as an AmeriCorps member through Virginia Campus Outreach Opportunity League (Virginia COOL). After several years of working for COOL, she became program director at the North Richmond Family YMCA. At the YMCA she worked closely with youth by coordinating a middle-school mentoring program, leading an adulthood curriculum, and working with an after-school program for girls. In 2001, she transitioned from the YMCA to the University of Richmond, where she worked for nine years. At the university, she developed programs that deepened student awareness regarding issues of socioeconomic class, race, gender, and sexual orientation.

STEPHANIE JONES

Stephanie Jones is associate professor in the department of educational theory and practice at the University of Georgia. Her research and teaching are focused on working-class and poor children and youth experiences inside and outside educational institutions. She is the author of *Girls, Social Class, and Literacy: What Teachers Can Do to Make a Difference* and has published widely in education journals.

JENNIFER LADD

Jennifer Ladd is an experienced coach, facilitator, philanthropic adviser, and diversity trainer working to support individuals and organizations. She began offering cross-class dialogue groups with Felice Yeskel in 2001 and founded Class Action in 2004. She has worked for over twenty-five years with people with earned and inherited wealth as part of her dedication to creating resilient community by helping resources move where they are most needed. Ladd has a doctorate in education and a master's in human development, and she has spent many years in elementary education and teacher training in the fields of global, cross-cultural communication and antibias education. She uses theater and art, as well as traditional tools and practices, to help organizations and individuals achieve their goals.

DWIGHT LANG

Dwight Lang teaches in the sociology department at the University of Michigan, where he focuses on issues of social class differences in higher education and the wider community. He is a faculty adviser to the undergraduate group First-Generation College Students @ Michigan, which gives those students an opportunity to gather on a regular basis to discuss issues of adjustment and achievement in a setting where most students come from middle- and upper-middle-class backgrounds. His contributions to the *Ann Arbor News*, including "The Collateral Damage of Class Warfare" (May 27, 2009) and "First Generation Students at Michigan Share Their Stories" (April 2013), discuss issues that first-generation students face. He also contributes op-eds to the *Detroit Free Press* addressing topics related to social class inequality, including "A Troubling Silence on Poverty" (November 2012). He is a member of the Association of Working Class Academics.

FISHER LAVELL

Fisher Lavell was born to a very poor, mixed-blood family in rural Manitoba, Canada. She has earned a master's degree and has published fiction in *Prairie Fire*. Her personal essay "On the Road to Find Out: Everyday Advice for Working-Class Mothers Returning to School" was accepted to the juried publication *The Illusion of Inclusion: Women in Post-Secondary Education*. Her "Gleanings of a White Poor Woman" was published in *The Womanist* and excerpted in Lorimer's *Canadian Women's Issues*. Still based in Manitoba, Lavell is a school counselor, serving predominantly working-class native Canadians. In her free time, she works on her first novel, *Roaring River Woman*. Soon she will return home and live in the little house her father built with his own hands.

BETSY LEONDAR-WRIGHT

Betsy Leondar-Wright grew up in an upper-middle-class white family in suburban New Jersey. She is the author of *Missing Class: Strengthening Social Movement Groups by Seeing Class Cultures* (Cornell University Press, 2014) and *Class Matters: Cross-Class Alliance Building for Middle-Class Activists* (2005), and she coauthored *The Color of Wealth: The Story behind the Racial Wealth Divide* (2006). She has a PhD in sociology and teaches about social movements and class and race inequality. A longtime economic justice activist, Leondar-Wright was the communications director of United for a Fair Economy from 1997 to 2006, and since 2010 she has been the program director at Class Action (www.classism.org).

JANET LIGHTFOOT

Janet Lightfoot was born into the culture of hunger and had parents who were unable to pay the rent. Born and raised in Maine and a longtime advocate for the poor, Lightfoot works with private agencies and fights government bureaucracies to deliver the resources government is legally required to provide. She currently lives, works, and advocates in Colorado Springs, Colorado.

CATHERINE ORLAND

Catherine Brenner Orland is a facilitator, trainer, and consultant who guides corporations, schools, and nonprofits in their attempts to strengthen and manage diversity. She holds a master of arts in social justice in intercultural relations from the School for International Training in Brattleboro, Vermont, and is the author of *Teachers, Study Circles and the Racial Achievement Gap*.

CHRISTINE OVERALL

Christine Overall is a professor and holds a research chair in the department of philosophy at Queen's University in Kingston, Ontario. She is the author of six books, including, most recently, *Why Have Children? The Ethical Debate* (2012). Her teaching and research focus on bioethics, social philosophy, and feminist theory.

PATIENCE RAGE

Patience Rage is a writer and storyteller in the Germantown section of Philadelphia, where she lives with her granddaughter, Ishaiah, and Susan, the love of her life. Her work ranges from mentoring groups of young black boys and men of color to painting houses to event organizing to writing and performing her stories. Her pieces have been published in *Aviary, City Paper,* and other publications. Her interests also include cultural competency workshops and cross-class dialogue groups. In 2005, she was awarded the Leeway Art and Change Grant for her work with women survivors of incest. She has a bachelor of arts from Goddard College.

CHARLOTTE REDWAY

Charlotte Redway lives in Portland, Oregon, where she works as a licensed clinical social worker in private practice and with families involved with child welfare. Her experience includes working in residential treatment, being an advocate at a domestic violence shelter, and counseling LGBT youth at the local queer youth organization. She received her master's in social work at the Smith College School for Social Work. Redway has been published in *Smith College Studies in Social Work* and contributed to various written projects produced by Resource Generation. She has presented at the "Making Money Make Change" conference on cross-class relationships and continues to address this issue in her work.

GENEVA REYNAGA-ABIKO

Geneva Reynaga-Abiko is a Mexican American cisgendered female whose grandparents immigrated to the United States when it was still legal to walk across the border. She is a licensed clinical psychologist who was the first person in her family to attend college. Originally from southern California, she has worked all over the United States, primarily in university counseling centers. She is currently the director of counseling services at the California Polytechnic State University in San Luis Obispo, California. Professionally, Reynaga-Abiko identifies as a feminist multiculturalist with specializations in diversity psychologies, particularly Latina/o psychology; LGBTQ psychology, including queer theories; intersectionality; and Buddhist psychology. She loves working with students and continues to supervise doctoral-level trainees in her current practice. Reynaga-Abiko is a member of several professional organizations and enjoys presenting and publishing whenever the opportunity arises.

JOHN ROSARIO-PEREZ

John Rosario-Perez is a psychologist and psychoanalyst practicing in Cambridge, Massachusetts. He is from a bicultural background (Puerto Rican and American), although he was raised mostly by his Anglo grandparents in the Southwest. A graduate of Brown University, he was a writer and journalist before becoming a psychologist. His fiction and nonfiction work have been published in the *Boston Globe, Tribe,* and the *Carolina Quarterly,* among others. He is a graduate of the Massachusetts Institute for Psychoanalysis and is on the staff of the Tufts University Counseling and Mental Health Service.

APRIL ROSENBLUM
April Rosenblum is a writer, educator, and activist in Philadelphia. Her work has appeared in *Bridges, New Voices,* and *Jewish Currents* and in the books *Righteous Indignation: A Jewish Call for Justice* and the *International Encyclopedia of Protest and Revolution.* In 2007, the *Jewish Forward* named her one of the fifty most influential Jews in the United States for her teaching tools for activists on anti-Semitism.

KAREN SPECTOR
Karen Spector is currently an assistant professor in the College of Education at the University of Alabama. She taught high school English in Florida and Ohio with diverse students before earning her doctorate in education in literacy from the University of Cincinnati. Her research has been published in journals such as *Research in the Teaching of English* and *Journal of Adolescent and Adult Literacy,* as well as in several books, including *Trajectories: Social and Educational Mobility of Education Scholars from Poor and Working Class Backgrounds.* In 2011, she coedited *Culturally Relevant Pedagogy: Clashes and Confrontations.*

LINDA STOUT
Linda Stout, founder of Spirit in Action, lives in North Carolina. A thirteenth-generation Quaker born into a tenant-farming family, Stout founded Piedmont Peace Project, a successful grassroots organization located in a conservative region of North Carolina. She and the organization forged extraordinary alliances across race and class lines and helped to initiate major public policy changes. A recipient of the Freedom Fighter Award of the Equal Rights Congress, Stout was featured in Studs Terkel's book *Hope Dies Last.* She is the author of *Bridging the Class Divide and Other Lessons for Grassroots Organizing,* and *Collective Visioning: Creating the World We Want to Live In,* published in 2011.

K. STRICKER
K. Stricker completed her PhD at Loyola University, Chicago, and is currently associate professor of teacher education at Concordia University in Chicago. Prior to that, Stricker taught high school social studies in South Dakota and Chicago.

MICHELLE M. TOKARCZYK

Michelle Tokarczyk grew up in the Bronx and Queens. Her father was a toll collector, and her mother was a homemaker. After graduating from a girls' Catholic high school, she attended Herbert Lehman College and went on for a PhD in English at SUNY Stony Brook. After four years in contingent teaching positions, she received a tenure-track appointment at Goucher College and is professor of English there. Tokarczyk is one of the founders of the field of working-class studies, former president of the Working-Class Studies Association, and has edited the widely cited *Working-Class Women in the Academy: Laborers in the Knowledge Factory*. Her most recent work, an edited anthology, *Critical Approaches to American Working-Class Literature*, was published in 2011.

POLLY TROUT

Polly Trout is the founder and executive director of Patacara Community Services, which is opening a donation-only cafe and community wellness center serving low income people in Seattle, Washington. Previously, Trout founded Seattle Education Access, a nonprofit that provides higher education advocacy and opportunity to people struggling to overcome poverty and adversity. She has a bachelor of arts from Evergreen State College, a master of theological studies from Harvard Divinity School, and a PhD in religious studies from Boston University.

JOHN VAUGHN

The Reverend John Vaughn currently serves as the executive vice president at Auburn Theological Seminary. The mission of Auburn is to inspire and equip bold and resilient leaders with the tools and resources they need—education, research, support, and media savvy—to bridge religious divides, build community, and pursue justice in our complex, multifaith, media-driven world. Vaughn is responsible for the overall planning and management of the seminary. Before joining Auburn, he served as the program director for the Twenty-First Century Foundation based in Harlem, a national foundation that advances strategic giving for black community change. His earlier positions included service as executive director of the Peace Development Fund, minister for education and social justice at the Riverside Church in New York City, and director for community development at the Community Training and Assistance Center (CTAC) in Boston. An ordained minister in the American Baptist Churches, Vaughn received his bachelor's degree from Holy Cross College and his master of divinity degree from the Pacific School of Religion in Berkeley, California.

WENDY WILLIAMS
Wendy R. Williams is an associate professor of psychology and women's studies at Berea College in Kentucky. She received her PhD in social psychology from the University of California, Santa Cruz, in 2005. Her research focuses on documenting the lived experiences of poor and working-class Americans and the personal and political consequences of how they are perceived by others. She recently coauthored an article in *Deconstructing Privilege: Teaching and Learning as Allies in the Classroom*, edited by Kim Case.

Resources

This is a short list of resources about class and classism. For up-to-date resources see www.classism.org.

BOOKS

Collins, Chuck. *99 to 1: How Wealth Inequality Is Wrecking the World and What We Can Do About It*. Berrett-Koehler, 2012.

Freeman, Pamela, and Phyllis Labanowski. *Created Equal: High School Curriculum on Class and Classism*. Class Action, 2012.

Greenberg, Zoe. *Enough*. DVD. Class Action, 2008.

hooks, bell. *Where We Stand: Class Matters*. Routledge, 2000.

Jensen, Barbara. *Reading Classes: On Culture and Classism in America*. Cornell University Press, 2012.

Ladd, Jennifer, Jerry Koch-Gonzalez, and Felice Yeskel. *Talking across the Class Divide: Cross-Class Dialogue Manual*. Class Action, 2008.

Leondar-Wright, Betsy. *Missing Class: Strengthening Social Movement Groups by Seeing Class Cultures*. Cornell University Press, 2014.

Lubrano, Al. *Limbo: Blue Collar Roots, White Collar Dreams*. John Wiley & Sons, 2003.

Lui, Meizhu, et al. *The Color of Wealth: The Story behind the U.S. Racial Wealth Divide*. New Press, 2006.

Shapiro, Thomas. *The Hidden Cost of Being African American: How Wealth Perpetuates Inequality*. Oxford University Press, 2004.

Stout, Linda. *Bridging the Class Divide and Other Lessons for Grassroots Organizing*. Beacon, 1996.

Tea, Michelle. *Without a Net: The Female Experience of Growing Up Working Class*. Seal Press, 2004.

Zweig, Michael. *The Working-Class Majority*. 2nd ed. Cornell University Press, 2011.

WEBSITES

www.classism.org
www.inequality.org
www.wealthinequality.org

About Class Action

C lass Action is a national nonprofit founded in 2004 by Jennifer Ladd and Felice Yeskel, two of the editors of this book, who grew up at different ends of the class spectrum and who wanted to end the silence and taboos against talking about socioeconomic class in our lives, workplaces, schools, and communities.

Class Action's mission is to inspire action to end classism. Class Action provides a dynamic framework for understanding class and inequality and an intersectional analysis of race and class through powerful interactive trainings, workshops, presentations, organizational consulting, and public education. For more information and resources visit www.classism.org.